Introducing HTML5 Game Development

Jesse Freeman

O'REILLY®

Beijing · Cambridge · Farnham · Köln · Sebastopol · Tokyo

Introducing HTML5 Game Development

by Jesse Freeman

Published by O'Reilly Media, Inc., 1005 Gravenstein Highway North, Sebastopol, CA 95472.

O'Reilly books may be purchased for educational, business, or sales promotional use. Online editions are also available for most titles (*http://my.safaribooksonline.com*). For more information, contact our corporate/institutional sales department: (800) 998-9938 or *corporate@oreilly.com*.

Editor: Mary Treseler
Development Editor: Kristin L. Kelly
Production Editor: Kristen Borg

Cover Designer: Karen Montgomery
Interior Designer: David Futato
Illustrator: Robert Romano

Revision History for the First Edition:
2012-02-10   First release
See *http://oreilly.com/catalog/errata.csp?isbn=9781449315177* for release details.

ISBN: 978-1-449-31517-7

[LSI]

1328895248

I would like to dedicate this book to Ed Love, who was my teacher, mentor, and good friend when I went to Florida State University. He was a very important person in my life and his sudden passing indirectly motivated me to explore computer art, which snowballed into what I do today.

Table of Contents

Preface

About This Book

This relatively short book attempts to cover a very large topic. While this book is considered an introduction to building HTML5 games with Impact, a JavaScript game framework, it is also intended to be a companion guide to help you get started making, and more importantly, finishing your games. I have created a high-level overview of what I consider to be the most important parts of making a game with Impact, along with what you should keep in mind or research further in order to become a better game developer. This book will take you step-by-step through the process of creating a 2D side-scrolling game with Impact, and how to publish it to the web and even package it up as a native iOS app.

I have also worked very hard to condense all this material as much as possible. That being said, when topics are larger than the scope of this book, I do my best to point you in the right direction so you can find more information. Making games is hard work and requires not only technical skills, but also a lot of planning and commitment to completing the project. While following this book may not guarantee a hit game, it will most certainly prepare you to complete the game you start, which any game developer will tell you is probably the hardest part.

Who This Book Is For

Introducing HTML5 Game Development is a book targeting all levels of game developers. Having prior programing knowledge (especially being familiar with JavaScript) doesn't hurt, but it's not necessarily a requirement. In this book, we will cover how Impact works and build the basic foundation of a game with it. We will also cover a little bit about game design and how to publish your Impact games to the Web, desktop, and mobile. For mobile deployment, we will look at how to publish your game as a native app on iOS devices.

Who This Book Is Not For

This book is not for developers who are looking to build fully cross-browser and mobile games with JavaScript. While HTML5 has come a long way in the past few years, we are still far away from widespread adoption of the underlying technologies Impact relies on, such as Canvas, sound, and advanced user input. That doesn't mean it isn't possible to make a cross-platform game with Impact but before we move on, I just want to set your expectations correctly. Impact requires modern browsers and even on mobile devices with browsers that support HTML5, you will still run into audio issues that may affect the ability of your game to run correctly for everyone.

Conventions Used in This Book

The following typographical conventions are used in this book:

Italic
: Indicates new terms, URLs, email addresses, filenames, and file extensions.

`Constant width`
: Used for program listings, as well as within paragraphs to refer to program elements such as variable or function names, databases, data types, environment variables, statements, and keywords.

`Constant width bold`
: Shows commands or other text that should be typed literally by the user.

`Constant width italic`
: Shows text that should be replaced with user-supplied values or by values determined by context.

 This icon signifies a tip, suggestion, or general note.

This Book's Example Files

You can download the example files for this book from this location:

> *http://examples.oreilly.com/0636920022633/*

In the example files, you will find all the files necessary for the book. In addition to the game source code, you will also find the source code for the iOS version of the final game. Since Impact's source code cannot be distributed with this book's examples, you will have to supply your own copy of Impact to make these examples work. Make sure you read the included *ReadMe.txt* file for information on what is included with the download and how to correctly set it up.

Using Code Examples

This book is here to help you get your job done. In general, you may use the code in this book in your programs and documentation. You do not need to contact us for permission unless you're reproducing a significant portion of the code. For example, writing a program that uses several chunks of code from this book does not require permission. Selling or distributing a CD-ROM of examples from O'Reilly books does require permission. Answering a question by citing this book and quoting example code does not require permission. Incorporating a significant amount of example code from this book into your product's documentation does require permission.

We appreciate, but do not require, attribution. An attribution usually includes the title, author, publisher, and ISBN. For example: "*Introducing HTML5 Game Development* by Jesse Freeman (O'Reilly). Copyright 2012 Game Cook, Inc., 978-1-4493-1517-7."

If you feel your use of code examples falls outside fair use or the permission given above, feel free to contact us at *permissions@oreilly.com*.

How To Use This Book

Development rarely happens in a vacuum. In today's world, email, Twitter, blog posts, coworkers, friends, and colleagues all play a vital role in helping you solve development problems. Consider this book yet another resource at your disposal to help you solve the development problems you will encounter. The content is arranged in such a way that solutions should be easy to find and easy to understand. However, this book does have a big advantage: it is available anytime of the day or night.

Safari® Books Online

Safari Books Online is an on-demand digital library that lets you easily search over 7,500 technology and creative reference books and videos to find the answers you need quickly.

With a subscription, you can read any page and watch any video from our library online. Read books on your cell phone and mobile devices. Access new titles before they are available for print, and get exclusive access to manuscripts in development and post feedback for the authors. Copy and paste code samples, organize your favorites, download chapters, bookmark key sections, create notes, print out pages, and benefit from tons of other time-saving features.

O'Reilly Media has uploaded this book to the Safari Books Online service. To have full digital access to this book and others on similar topics from O'Reilly and other publishers, sign up for free at *http://my.safaribooksonline.com*.

How to Contact Us

Please address comments and questions concerning this book to the publisher:

O'Reilly Media, Inc.
1005 Gravenstein Highway North
Sebastopol, CA 95472
800-998-9938 (in the United States or Canada)
707-829-0515 (international or local)
707-829-0104 (fax)

We have a web page for this book, where we list errata, examples, and any additional information. You can access this page at:

http://shop.oreilly.com/product/0636920022633.do

To comment or ask technical questions about this book, send email to:

bookquestions@oreilly.com

For more information about our books, courses, conferences, and news, see our website at *http://www.oreilly.com*.

Find us on Facebook: *http://facebook.com/oreilly*

Follow us on Twitter: *http://twitter.com/oreillymedia*

Watch us on YouTube: *http://www.youtube.com/oreillymedia*

Acknowledgments

First and foremost, I would like to thank my wife and son for all their support while I was making this book. I'd also like to thank my parents and family for all their help and support over the years. I also have a lot of respect for all the thought leaders in the development community who continue to inspire me, such as Keith Peters, John Lindquist, Jesse Warden, Chuck Freedman, Sean McCracken, Michael Labriola, Nate Beck, Troy Gilbert, Joel Hooks, Brendan Lee, Scott Penberthy, Seb Lee-Delisle, Rich Shupe, and especially Jobe Makar who taught me how to make Flash games years ago.

Thank you as well to Mary Treseler and Rich Tretola from O'Reilly Media, Inc., for providing me with this opportunity and to Dominic Szablewski for his feedback on this book and for creating such a great game framework. I also couldn't have done this book without the help from my amazing tech editors: Riche Shupe, Gareth Parker and Richard Davey.

Finally I wanted to give a special thanks to Dan Wolfe for creating the splash screen art for Resident Raver, as well as for his artistic help on my other games. And I can't forget my good friend Frank Pirozzi for inspiring me to create Resident Raver and shoot a video of it back in college.

CHAPTER 1

Introduction To Impact

Impact is a JavaScript game framework created by Dominic Szablewski. Impact takes advantage of the modern browser's Canvas element in order to create high-performance 2D games on the Web and even mobile. One of the biggest advantages of using Impact is that it is easy to pick up, comes with very good code examples, has an active community, and has a very robust level editor called Weltmeister. The only barrier of entry is the licensing fee for the software, since it is not open source. After purchasing a license, you do get the full source code, the Weltmeister level editor, and free current major version updates (1.x). While there are other open source and free JavaScript game frameworks out there, Impact has an extra level of polish I haven't seen with anything else so far.

Why Use Impact?

Perhaps one of the most appealing factors of buying Impact is the inclusion of a sample Objective-C project that allows you to compile your Web game into a native iOS app. This enables your game to take advantage of OpenGL for graphics and OpenAL for sound instead of the Canvas and Audio elements in the mobile Safari browser. This solution gives your game almost native-like performance on iOS, and it can be packaged up and sold in the Apple Store just like a native app.

Here are some links to help you learn more about Impact and examples of it in action:

Site: *http://impactjs.com*
Forum: *http://impactjs.com/forums*
Demos: *http://impactjs.com/forums/games*
Purchase: *http://impactjs.com/buy-impact*

Tools you will need:

PHP
> For saving levels created with Weltmeister.

Apache
> For locally hosting and testing your game.

IDEs
> Impact has no IDE dependencies; you can create your games with any simple text editor. I prefer to use WebStorm or PHPStorm since these IDEs, which are made by JetBrains, offer code hinting, project management, refactoring, and debugging.

Browsers
> Impact works very well on WebKit browsers, especially Chrome, but any modern browser with support for Canvas and the Audio tag should also work.

Setting Up a Local Environment

Before getting started, we are going to have to set up a simple Web development environment in order to take full advantage of Impact and its level editor. Plus, by setting up a local development environment, we can simulate what it will be like to host the game in a production environment. Let's take a look at configuring Apache, the IDE, and Impact itself.

Install WebStorm/PHPStorm

While you can use any basic text editor, I prefer to use an IDE that offers a more robust set of features such as code hinting, refactoring, project management, version control integration, and a debugger. JetBrains has two IDEs that both handle JavaScript/HTML5 development. If you only plan on doing JavaScript development, I would suggest using WebStorm. If you need to do HTML5 and PHP development (which comes in handy since Impact's level editor uses PHP) you should look at PHPStorm.

Installing these applications is straightforward. Here are URLs for each IDE:

WebStorm
> http://www.jetbrains.com/webstorm

PHPStorm
> http://www.jetbrains.com/phpstorm

Each IDE has a 30-day trial and after the trial costs $99 for a license. There are a lot of resources out there on how to use each IDE, so I am not going to cover it here.

Install Apache/PHP/MySQL

There are many guides for installing Apache and PHP on your operating system of choice. Here are some simple one-click solutions to help get you up and running as quickly as possible:

Mac

For Mac, you should use an all-in-one solution such as **MAMP** (*http://www.mamp .info/en/index.html*). This is a free one-click solution for getting Apache, PHP, and MySQL set up on your Mac. Likewise, you can also use the built-in version of PHP that comes with OS X, but you will need to do some manual configuration of Apache to get it working. Simply do a search for "Enabling PHP in Mac OS X" in order to find instructions.

PC

Just like on Mac, there are some excellent one-click solutions for setting up Apache, PHP, and MySQL. I have used **XAMP** (*http://www.apachefriends.org/en/xampp .html*) in the past, and have had excellent success with it.

Other Hosting Options

If you prefer not to work on a LAMP (Linux, Apache, MySQL, PHP) stack you can check out the following projects that allow you to run Impact on different hosting environments:

Node.js

Conner Petzold made a Node.js module that allows Impact to run on a Node HTTP server. His Node-Impact module is on GitHub at *https://github.com/cpetzold/node -impact*.

.NET

You can run Impact on IIS and .NET thanks to Mike Hamilton's ImpactJS-IIS-.NET-API project, which you can find at *http://code.google.com/p/impactjs-iis -backend*.

Ruby

Chris Darroch put together a Sinatra backend for Impact. Just remove the .php extensions for the API calls in your `lib/weltmeister/config.js` and fire up `impact.rb`, which you can find at *https://github.com/chrisdarroch/impactrb*.

Python

Joe Esposito has a GitHub project that implements a backend server in Python for Impact to let you develop multiple games at once. You can check out the project at *https://github.com/joeyespo/py-impactjs*.

Setting Up a New Impact Project

Impact is a self-contained project. Each game you create will require you to copy the default Impact project folder (which you get once you buy a license) into a new location on your server and start from scratch. Impact is set up so you can easily do all your work from your local host.

To get started, copy the Impact project into your local host. You should see the following files (Figure 1-1).

Figure 1-1. Impact project files.

As you can see, I have renamed my `impact` folder `residentraver`, which is the name of the game we are going to create in this book. Here is a quick breakdown of everything in the folder:

index.html
> This is the main .html file that runs your game.

lib
> This is the core code for Impact and where you will store your own game-specific JS files. This also contains the source code for Weltmeister.

media
> This is the assets directory, and where all game art and sound files will go.

tools
> This directory contains .php scripts to minify your game's JS files and make it harder for people to have access to the game's source code. This is part of the license and is important so you don't accidentally distribute the source code.

weltmeister.html
> This is the level editor's .html file.

You should now have everything you need to run your first game. If you open your browser and navigate to *http://localhost/residentraver*[1] you should see the following page (Figure 1-2).

---

1. Based on how Apache is set up on your computer, you may have a different URL for your localhost. If you are using MAMP, it may be http://localhost:8888, or with XAMP it is http://localhost. Refer to your Apache documentation for the correct URL.

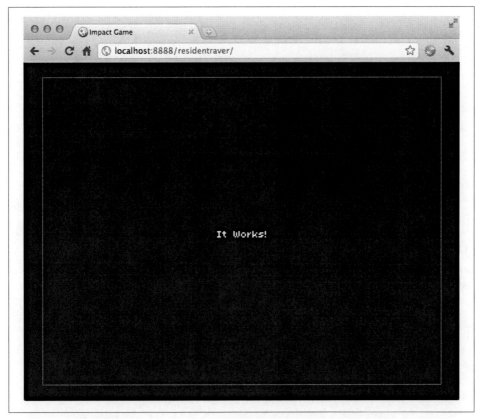

Figure 1-2. This is what you will see when you run an Impact game for the first time.

Before moving on, I just wanted to take a quick moment to look at the *index.html* file and how it is set up. Open it up in your editor and you should see the following HTML code:

```
1   <!DOCTYPE html>
2   <html>
3   <head>
4       <title>Impact Game</title>
5       <style type="text/css">
6           html,body {
7               background-color: #000;
8               color: #fff;
9               font-family: helvetica, arial, sans-serif;
10              margin: 0;
11              padding: 0;
12              font-size: 12pt;
13          }
14
```

```
15          #canvas {
16              position: absolute;
17              left: 0;
18              right: 0;
19              top: 0;
20              bottom: 0;
21              margin: auto;
22              border: 1px solid #555;
23          }
24      </style>
25
26      <script type="text/javascript" src="lib/impact/impact.js"></script>
27      <script type="text/javascript" src="lib/game/main.js"></script>
28  </head>
29  <body>
30      <canvas id="canvas"></canvas>
31  </body>
32  </html>
```

Outside of the style tag, you may notice there isn't a lot of code actually embedded in the page. We have two script tags that load in the impact.js framework and our main.js JavaScript file. Finally the only tag in body is the Canvas element.

The Canvas element is part of the HTML5 spec and is what actually allows Impact to run in the browsers. Think of the canvas as an image that we can draw bitmap data into. Impact takes care of all the underlying code we would have had to write in order to display game graphics to the screen. You can learn more about how the Canvas tag works at *http://www.whatwg.org/specs/web-apps/current-work/multipage/the -canvas-element.html#the-canvas-element*. It's also important to note that the Canvas element only works in modern browsers such as Chrome 13+, Safari 3.2+, Firefox 6+ and IE 9+. For a full list of browsers that support the Canvas element, go to *http://caniuse.com/#search=can vas*.

You can also add your own HTML code around the Canvas element and design this page to look like any other HTML file. Just keep in mind that we use the canvas id in our game in order to tell impact where to render our game's graphics to, so don't change it unless you update your game's initialization logic.

Now we are ready to learn more about the Impact framework.

Modules

Impact's source code is organized into modules. Since JavaScript itself does not have an include() function that can load other JavaScript source files into an object, Impact has its own system. A module typically looks like this:

```
1    ig.module(
2        'game.my-file'
3    )
4    .requires(
5        'impact.game',
6        'impact.image',
7        'game.other-file'
8    )
9    .defines(function(){
10       // code for this module
11   });
```

The first block defines the module name 'game.my-file', which directly corresponds to the file name. Modules and their dependencies typically reside in the lib/ folder of your Impact project directory, and subdirectories are included in a path to these files using object-model dot syntax. Therefore, the my-file.js file sits in the lib/game/my-file.js.

The second block defines any additional files that will be loaded at runtime. Since JavaScript itself does not have an established way to load other JavaScript source files into an object, Impact has its own system. The modules listed in the .requires() method will be loaded from the lib/impact/game.js, lib/impact/image.js, and lib/game/other-file.js project directory, respectively. These required files will be loaded before the module's body and before the last block of the above module example is executed.

The last step the module takes is to execute the function passed to the .defines() method. This linear process allows you to control when code is loaded and run. It's important to follow Impact's file naming and location structure since it will try to automatically load these resources for you during the pre-load phase. Next, we'll talk a little more about classes in Impact and how they work.

How Classes Work

In JavaScript, there is no real notion of a traditional class structure like you have in other OOP languages. In JavaScript, everything is an Object. While this allows JavaScript to be incredibly flexible, it also makes it difficult to structure your code in a reusable way. To solve this issue, Impact has a pseudo-class object, which is the basis of every class we will create in our game.

 Impact's class object is based on John Resig's simple JavaScript inheritance code (*http://ejohn.org/blog/simple-javascript-inheritance*), but it is extended with deep copying of properties and static instantiation.

Here is an example of how we can create a new person class by building off of Impact's core Class object:

```
1    // Create a new class "Person"
2    var Person = ig.Class.extend({
3        name: '',
4        init: function( name ) {
5            this.name = name;
6        }
7    });
8
9    // Instantiate an object of the first class
10   var e = new Person('John Doe');
11   e.name; // => John Doe
```

You may have noticed that we actually extend the functionality of the **ig.Class** object via the .extend() method.

 In traditionally class based languages, the extends keyword allows us to copy over the existing functionality of another class. This is what will allow us to infuse additional functionality into all of our game classes without having to actually duplicate code all over the place.

In addition to extending off of **ig.Class**, you can actually extend off of any custom class you create. Again, in order to extend another class you simply use the .extend() functionality. Here we are going to extend off of our person class to create a new zombie class:

```
1    // Create another class by extending the "Person" class
2    var Zombie = Person.extend({
3        init: function( name ) {
4            this.parent( 'Zombie: ' + name );
5        }
6    });
7
8    // Instantiate an object of the second class
9    var p = new Zombie('John Doe');
10   p.name; // => Zombie: John Doe
```

All classes that are created with .extend() will also have an .extend() method that can be used for further subclassing. When working inside of extended classes, you can use .this and .parent for scope. You will see later on how splitting up core logic into individual classes will help expostulate functionality and make our game code easier to maintain while we develop it.

Core Classes

Impact is made up of several core classes that revolve around the game framework and all the necessary systems such as rendering, maps, sounds, and more. All the classes are in the **ig** namespace, which is set up by the core class. Here is a list of the main classes used in Impact along with a short description of what they do:

---

ig Core

The **ig** object provides the module definition and loading capabilities as well as some utility functions.

Animation

An **ig.Animation** object takes care of animating an entity or BackgroundMap tiles. Frames from an **AnimationSheet**—an image with all animation frames—are drawn as specified by the animation's **frameTime** and sequence.

AnimationSheet

ig.AnimationSheet is a thin wrapper around an **ig.Image** object. It specifies the **width** and **height** properties for each animation frame in the sheet. It is used by the **ig.Animation** class.

BackgroundMap

An **ig.BackgroundMap** draws tiles from a Tileset, as indicated by its 2D data array.

CollisionMap

An **ig.Collision** takes a 2D TileMap and allows tracing against it for collisions.

Entity

Interactive objects in the game world are typically subclassed from this base entity class. It provides animation, drawing, and basic physics. Subclassing your entities from **ig.Entity** ensures that it can be added to the game world, react to the CollisionMap along with other entities, and be added to a level within Weltmeister.

Font

An **ig.Font** object loads a specially formatted font image and allows you to draw text with it.

Game

ig.Game is the main hub for your game. It hosts all currently active entities, BackgroundMaps, and a CollisionMap. You can subclass your own game class from **ig.Game**.

Image

ig.Image is a wrapper around image resources (.png, .gif, .jpeg). It takes care of loading and scaling the source image. You can draw the whole image by calling **.draw()** or just one tile of it by calling **.drawTile()**.

Input

ig.Input handles all keyboard and mouse input.

Loader

ig.Loader is the default pre-loader for all images and sounds that the game needs. By default, it displays a white progress bar on a black background.

Map

ig.Map is the base class for **ig.BackgroundMap** and **ig.CollisionMap**. It only provides basic access to the tiles in the map data.

Music

ig.Music offers the ability to play a list of background music in order or randomly.

Sound

An instance of ig.Sound represents a sound file to be used as background music or game sound.

SoundManager

The SoundManager takes care of loading sounds and providing them for ig.Music and ig.Sound instances. An instance of the SoundManager is automatically created at ig.soundManager by the ig.main() function.

System

ig.System takes care of starting and stopping the run loop and calls the .run() method on the current game object. It also does the housekeeping for ig.Input and provides some utility methods.

Timer

The ig.Timer has two distinct modes of operation. You can either get the difference by calling .delta() between the current time and the timer's target time (as set by the constructor or .set()) or just get the current tick—the time since the last call to .tick().

You can learn more about each of these classes and their methods on Impact's website under the documentation section at *http://impactjs.com/documentation*.

How Inner Classes Work

In traditional class-based languages, you usually have the option to put a class inside of another class's package structure. These are called inner classes. Impact has its own version of this, which allows us to add more than one class to a single module file.

Creating an inner class is similar to making a normal class, with the exception that you will be adding it to the end of the main class's module. These inner classes also support inheritance as well. Here is a quick example of two classes in the same module:

```
1   ig.module(
2       game.entities.myclass'
3   )
4   .requires(
5       'impact.entity'
6   )
7   .defines(function(){
8       EntityMyClass = ig.Entity.extend({
9           //Properties and methods go here
10          });
11
12      EntityMyInnerClass = ig.Entity.extend({
13          //Properties and methods go here
14          });
15  });
```

This technique is incredibly helpful when it comes to keeping your code organized, as you will see later in the book.

Level Editor

One of the best features of Impact is its level editor called Weltmeister. It is located in the libs/weltmeister folder inside the Impact project. We will go through using this editor in the next chapter, but I wanted to take some time to highlight its features and how to use it.

You can pull up the level editor anytime by navigating to the root of your project's domain and loading the weltmeister.html file. You will be presented with this screen:

Figure 1-3. This is the screen you will see after loading Weltmeister for the first time. Select a layer to see the grid numbers.

When you load the editor for the first time, you are presented with an empty untitled.js map file. Along the top are your main controls such as Save, Save As, New, and Load. Reload Images allows you to make visual tweaks to your map without having to do a hard refresh. Finally, on the far right, you will see a large arrow that shows/hides the layers, and below that are your map's layers. By default, there is an entities layer, which is where your player, monster, and other in-game elements will go. You can add new layers at any time by pressing the plus sign on the right of the Layers label.

 Layers simply allow you to draw level tiles onto the stage just as you would use a stamp tool in a painting program. If your game's level is incredibly detailed, you may want to break out parts of the level's tiles into a background, middle ground, and foreground layers as well as creating other layers for collision detection and additional details. Anything that moves in the game will go into the entities layer.

Before we can start making levels for our game, we need to create some graphics. Let's take a look at the asset pipeline, and more importantly, how to create graphics for Impact projects.

CHAPTER 2

Working With Sprites

Traditionally in gaming, the asset pipeline refers to the visual workflow you create for your project. This could be as simple as copying files over by hand into your game's media folder or writing more complex automation scripts to generate the art for you. For Impact games, all the in-game graphics are going to be sprites.

Sprites and Sprite Sheets

Sprites are the primary way we display and animate artwork in Impact games. A sprite is a single bitmap image that is drawn to the display—in this case the HTML5 Canvas element. To help organize them better, related sprites are grouped together into a single image called a sprite sheet.

Figure 2-1. An example of a sprite sheet from the game we are going to build.

Figure 2-1 shows a sprite sheet that contains all the visual states used for movement of the main character. Sprite sheets are usually set up using dimensions and coordinates that are easily divided. In this example, the sprite sheet is 160×16 pixels, and each sprite is 16×16 pixels. This allows us to simply divide the sprite sheet by 16 and automatically figure out that there are 10 sprites. Generally, when using sprite sheets for animation, we would tell the game engine which sprite is part of each animation set. Here is an example of how that will work in Impact:

```
this.addAnim( 'idle', 1, [0] );
this.addAnim( 'run', 0.07, [0,1,2,3,4,5] );
this.addAnim( 'jump', 1, [9] );
this.addAnim( 'fall', 0.4, [6,7] );
```

As you can see in this example, sprite 0 is our idle animation while 0-5 represents our run animations. We will explore setting up sprite animations a little later on when we begin setting up our game.

It's important to note that JavaScript's Arrays are zero-based, so our first sprite is always going to be 0, with each sprite increasing in value from there.

Sprite sheets are also good for non-animated graphics such as tiles for a level.

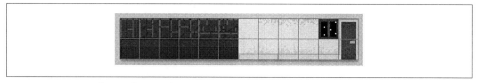

Figure 2-2. Sprites that make up a level are called Tilesets.

So, instead of registering animations manually, we can tell the game engine which tiles represent walls, decorations, or any other art you would need for your level's design.

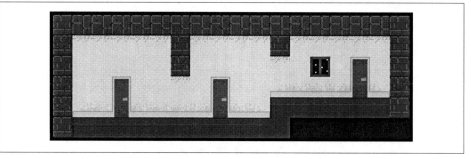

Figure 2-3. An image from Impact's level editor showing how these tiles are used in the game.

Now that we have a basic understanding of sprite sheets, let's look at how to actually create them for our games.

 When it comes to creating sprites for pixel-based games, there are several great image editors available for you to use. In this book we cover Photoshop but you should also check out GrafX2 (*http://code.google .com/p/grafx2/*) and GIMP (*http://www.gimp.org/*), which are free.

Scripting in Photoshop

Photoshop has several ways to build automation scripts, but for now we are just going to focus on using JavaScript. Basically, we will write a script that loops through the layers of the PSD, aligns each of the sprites in a row, and allows us to output a single file. One of the most important parts of generating graphics for games is picking the correct file format, color palette, and optimization settings by hand for each sprite sheet.

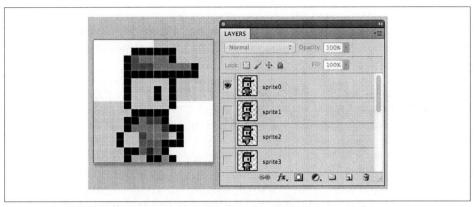

Figure 2-4. Our game's main character with each sprite animation on its own layer.

Photoshop scripts are simple text files saved as .js files. Usually, these scripts should be placed in the Presets/Scripts directory of your Photoshop installation folder. For simplicity, you can just manually run them by going into File→Scripts→Browse. In your script editor of choice, create a file called LayersToSprite.js and save it to your computer somewhere that is easy to find. Add the following code to your script:

```
1    // Arrange layers into a sprite sheet.
2    if (documents.length > 0)
3    {
4        docRef = activeDocument;
5        var activeLayer = docRef.activeLayer;
6
7        numLayers = docRef.artLayers.length;
8        var cols = docRef.width;
9
10       var spriteX = docRef.width;
11
12       // put things in order
13       app.preferences.rulerUnits = Units.PIXELS;
14
15       // resize the canvas
16       newX = numLayers * spriteX;
17
18       docRef.resizeCanvas(newX, docRef.height, AnchorPosition.TOPLEFT);
19
20       // move the layers around
21       for (i=0; i < numLayers; i++)
22       {
23           docRef.artLayers[i].visible = 1;
24           var movX = spriteX*i;
25           docRef.artLayers[i].translate(movX, 0);
26       }
27   }
```

Now that we have our script ready, let's open the `player.psd`, which is included in the books resources in the psds directory, in Photoshop and run the script to test that it works. When the script is done running, you will end up with something like Figure 2-5.

Figure 2-5. Our player sprite sheet, which was generated by the Photoshop script.

 In our game we actually use a PSD of our player with different types of weapons. You can find this additional file, along with the sprites for our zombie, in the psds directory if you also want to test the sprite sheet creation script on those files too. I have already gone ahead and created the final sprite sheets for the player and zombie in the media directory we will use for our game.

Congratulations, you have just created one of the most important tools for speeding up your sprite creation. Imagine how long it would take to do all of this by hand or, even worse, when changes happen—you would have to manually recreate all of these sheets each time. Scripting in Photoshop can get very complex, and it's good to read up on what you can actually do with it. While scripting in Photoshop may not be the most glamorous way to spend your time, I am sure you can agree that removing the repetitive nature of asset preparation is well worth the time investment.

If you are interested in learning more about Photoshop scripting, make sure to check out the following resource from Adobe:

http://www.adobe.com/devnet/photoshop/scripting.html

Working with Sprites in Photoshop

When it comes to working with sprites and tiles in Photoshop, it is important to set up your grid and guides to help get a better sense of the dimensions of each tile, especially when there is a lot of transparent space around the sprite. You can easily do this by going into Photoshop's Preferences menu and selecting Guides, Grid, & Slices... (Figure 2-6).

From here, you can set the guide size to match your sprite tile size. For our game, all the sprites are 16×16 or 8×8 pixels. By setting the subdivisions to 2, we will be able to see grids that work with our character sprites and level tiles as well (Figure 2-7).

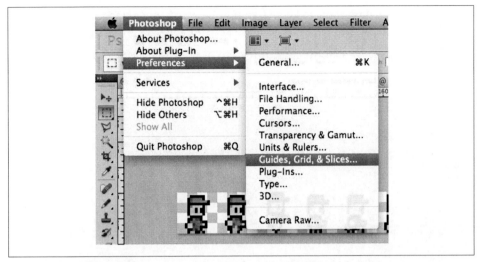

Figure 2-6. The menu where you will set the guide size to match your sprite tile size.

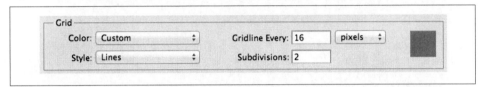

Figure 2-7. How to navigate the Photoshop Preferences menu to set your grid and guides.

Once you set this up, just turn on grid view from View→Show→Grid. You can also set auto-snapping to the grid, which may help align sprites more easily.

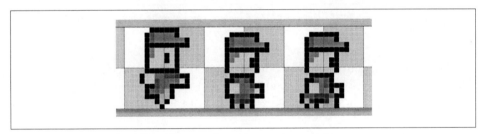

Figure 2-8. Now you should be able to see the grid around your sprite.

Optimizing Sprites

Now that we have our script for generating sprite sheets, we should talk about optimizing them. Impact is really good at working with 8-bit and pixelated artwork. That doesn't mean that you have to use this style for your own games but, if you do, there are a lot of great optimization tricks you can use in order to cut down on the file size of your assets. It's important to keep in mind that every single image of your game is loaded at run time, so you will want to make sure the file sizes are as small as possible.

In order to do this, we can use a great feature of Photoshop called Save for Web & Devices.

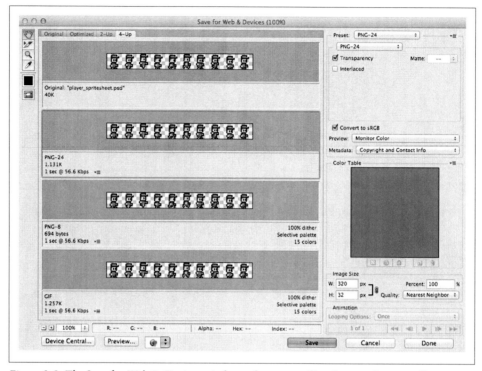

Figure 2-9. The Save for Web & Devices window, where you will make sure that your file sizes are as small as possible.

As you can see, the output window offers you several ways to preview the file size of different file compression types. I tend to use GIF or PNG-8 for simple artwork with no complex transparency. I use PNG-24 only when I have to. Remember, every KB counts.

CHAPTER 3

Introduction To Game Design

Before we jump in and start building our game, I want to cover the basics of game design.

What is Game Design?

When we talk about game design, we are not referring to the visual style of the game, but the actual gameplay mechanics themselves. Game design in its own right is an art form, and probably one of the most challenging parts of making any game. This is where you take an idea and not only transform it into a physical game that others can play, but also make sure the game is fun and well-balanced. The first step to designing a game usually starts with a game design document (GDD).

GDDs come in many shapes and sizes. Some people scribble them down in notebooks as drawings or use index cards. More traditionally, this is a multi-page text document containing the general concept of a game and its core mechanics that attempts to answer some basic questions about how the actual game works. At the very least, it should give the reader a clear idea of how the game will work and feel.

The GDD is critical for people getting started with making games because, without the experience of multiple games under your belt, it is easy to create something so complex and time-consuming that you will never be able to finish it. The GDD helps keep you on track and is an anchor to the core values of your original idea. This doesn't mean that it is set in stone, but thinking through as much of the interaction as possible before writing any code will go a long way toward helping you complete your game.

There are many books on the subject, and I will list some recommended reading at the end of the chapter. For now, here are a few key points I think are helpful to have in your GDD:

Start your document with a high concept

This is a term that is borrowed from the film industry and usually represents a "what if" scenario. When drafting a GDD, I tend to use a high concept to outline what the game is and its scenario, as well as outline any games that may already exist to draw inspiration from. Likewise, you can do a traditional high concept such as "What if we take Mario, but make him into a worm with a gun?" Asking these kinds of questions has been the inspirational fodder for many games for the past 30 years.

Try to add illustrations, sketches, and even more polished concept art to your document

It always helps to see what things will look like in your game. Games are very visual by nature; most people get bored out of their minds reading a 15-page or more design document with no indication of the artistic style you are envisioning for the game. Even worse, you leave that interpretation up to the reader's own imagination, so when they start seeing the first round of art concepts, it may be totally different from the impression they got from your doc. Designing a game is a very creative process, and you should have fun with it by sketching out as much as you can ahead of time.

Have a clear outline of the game's mechanics, how things work, and how they will interact with each other

Go into as much detail as possible around actions such as how combat works, leveling up, stats, rewards, etc.

Clearly illustrate how objects in your game are built

Include things like what properties a game actor may have such as life, weapon values, and more. This will be incredibly helpful when you go into development as a point of reference.

Don't worry about putting in too much

It's always better to start big and scale down as needed. The last thing you want to do is limit your imagination or creativity. Plus, you never know if the ideas you cut out for version one of your game could be reused in a follow-up game.

Finally, one of the most important things to do with your GDD is share it with as many people as possible. I know this goes against what you may feel is right, especially if you are afraid that people will steal your idea and take it for themselves. Obviously, I wouldn't share these ideas publicly on a website or social network (unless you are comfortable doing that), but find a core group of friends to bounce ideas off of. I use Google Docs to write my GDDs and share them with all my friends. It's a great collaborative platform because everyone can leave notes in your document and offer an outside insight if your game ideas need more work.

Sample Game Design Document

When it comes to personal projects, I start by outlining the core mechanics of a game or my general idea of what I would like to build, then start to add more and more detail as I work out how everything should operate. I have included one of my own GDDs for an RPG I have been working on called Tile Crusader. I have edited this down from my original document, as it was more than 20 pages long. Since RPGs are probably one of the most complex types of games to make, I find that having an organized and detailed GDD is essential for helping keep track of all the game systems you will end up having to build. Let's take a look at the scaled down version of Tile Crusader's GDD.

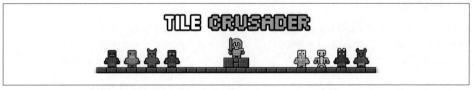

Figure 3-1. This graphics shows off the player and other monsters in the game, and is useful for helping set the tone of the GDD for first time readers.

Tile Crusader is a crowd-sourced, coffee break, rogue-like game that gives anyone the ability to pick up and play a random crusade in just a couple of minutes. The goal of Tile Crusader is to be a very casual RPG that is perfect to play in between boring tasks at work, while waiting for water to boil, or when you have some down-time. There is little time investment since there is no need to worry about spending hours building up a character. Tile Crusader is designed to be a quick and fun RPG experience!

Gameplay

Tile Crusader is a simple turn-based dungeon crawler. Each game revolves around completing a specific goal like kill all monsters, kill a boss, find an artifact, or simply escape. Tile Crusader is highly streamlined with simplified gameplay to offer the fastest experience possible. Monsters don't move in the game, so the player can choose when to engage in combat. Also, since other users create the maps, there are endless possibilities for new crusades to explore.

Exploring a Map

As the player explores the map, tiles are revealed to show monsters and treasure chests. The player uses the arrow keys to navigate the map. The player can interact with any object by colliding with it. When the player hits a treasure chest, it opens to reveal a pile of gold, a potion, a trap, or nothing. When the player collides with a monster, combat commences. Once the objective of a map is completed, the player can return to the exit and leave the level. Each tile the player reveals will be recoded, and at the end of a level, a bonus will be rewarded.

Combat

Tile Crusader is based on a point combat system. Combatants have an attack value and defense value. If the attack value is higher than the defending value, the difference is subtracted from the defending character's life. The attack and defend values are range-based, so there is some random chance the final value will be lower than the base attack value or a total miss. The player can leave combat at any time by walking away. Some monsters, such as bosses, will regenerate their health once you leave combat and as they go off-screen.

Completing a Map

When the player completes a map, they get to keep everything they find. If they die, they lose all their money and potions. Once the player completes a map, they are taken to an upgrade screen and, once the upgrades are completed, they can move onto the next random map.

Death

When a player dies, they restart the level and their stats/inventory is reset. Each death is recorded on a tombstone for that level. In addition to starting over, their character stats keep track of how many times the player has died in the game. This stat is not reset when a new game or character is created.

Main Character

When you create a new character, you can choose a class. Each class has skills and base starting stats. This is based on a point system, so each character is only allocated 20 points to be distributed in each property. Here is a list of classes:

Class	Max Life	Attack	Defense	Potions	Inventory
Knight	9	3	2	2	4
Mage	5	2	4	5	4
Thief	7	2	1	2	8

Monsters

There are nine types of monsters in the game. As the player finds monsters on the map, they will see an attack and defense value in order to gauge how difficult it will be to defeat them. Once a monster is defeated, it will be removed from the map and the player will gain a point to their kill score. If the map allows monsters to drop treasure, they may leave behind something from the treasure pool. It's also important to note that monsters do not move.

Sprite	Monster Type	Name	Sprite	Monster Type	Name
	Monster 1	Ork		Monster 6	Mummy
	Monster 2	Ogre		Monster 7	Skeleton
	Monster 3	Goblin		Monster 8	Imp
	Monster 4	Wolfman		Monster 9	Gargoyle
	Monster 5	Vampire			

Bosses

In game modes where the player has to defeat a boss, they must find them and kill them before they can leave the level. Bosses are always more powerful than the character, so make sure you are prepared to fight to the death in order to leave. There can be more than one boss per level.

Equipment

The player and monsters have equipment. Equipment consists of weapons, armor, helmets, and shields. Each piece of equipment modifies the character it is equipped to. Equipment has the following properties:

Property	Description
Name	Name of the item.
Type	Used to classify item: weapon, armor, helmet, shield, etc.
Modify	Name of the property to modify.

Inventory

The player has 12 possible inventory slots, two equippable slots (weapon and armor), and one dedicated slot for potions. Each player class has its own limitations on how much it can carry. When an item is equipped, it goes into the equippable slot. The player can only equip one weapon at a time and several types of armor. Armor is stacked into the armor slot so the player is allowed one piece of armor, a helmet, and a shield.

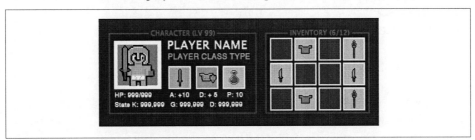

Figure 3-2. Tile Crusader HUD showing off player stats and inventory.

Equipping Items

When an item is equipped, it is placed in the player's weapon or armor slot. The modifier value for the item is displayed underneath it. Armor is stacked in the armor slot to show helmets, shield, and armor in one area.

Weapons and Armor

Each weapon and piece of armor in the game has four properties:

Property	Description
Name	Name of the weapon.
Base Value	Base value of the weapon; this modifies the attack property.
Graphic	This is the sprite ID to use for the weapon's graphic.
Type	This defines what slot an item is equipped to: weapon, armor, shield, helmet, etc.

This is a list of all the weapons in the game:

Sprite	Name	Base Value	Sprite	Name	Base Value
	Club	1		Hammer	4
	Dagger	2		Axe	5
	Mace	3		Sword	6

This is a list of all the shields in the game:

Sprite	Name	Base Value	Sprite	Name	Base Value
	Round Shield	2		Oval Shield	5
	Warrior Shield	3		Long Shield	7

This is a list of all the helmets in the game:

Sprite	Name	Base Value	Sprite	Name	Base Value
	Bucket Helmet	2		Full Helmet	5
	Roman Helmet	3		Fuller Helmet	7

This is a list of all the armor in the game:

Sprite	Name	Base Value	Sprite	Name	Base Value
	Light Chainmail	1		Chest Armor	5
	Chainmail	2		Full Armor	7

Leveling Up

The player is automatically leveled up when a crusade is completed. Not only do they increase a level, they also have the option to update one of the five main character properties: life, attack, health, potions, or inventory.

Winning the Game

There is no true way to win the game outside of staying alive. When the character dies, the player's game is over. Other than that, the goal is to stay alive for as long as you can across as many crusades as possible. When the player completes their mission, the crusade is over. The player gets to keep all of the items they found from the level, and collect a reward based on how well they did.

Coming Up With Ideas

Sometimes the hardest part of creating a game is just coming up with an idea. Or, maybe you have a lot of ideas and need to be able to focus on one of them. There are a few techniques I use to inspire me in my own games that help teach me important game mechanics we sometimes take for granted after playing games for a long time:

Keep a game journal

This doesn't have to be a traditional sketchbook (although that helps), but just something around where you can write down your game ideas. As I mentioned earlier, I use Google Docs to write all my game ideas when I have them. This way, I can come back to them when I have free time and flesh them out. Some game developers create elaborate sketches to work out their ideas, while others simply use sticky notes. There is no right or wrong way to go about this as long as you find a good system for jotting down your ideas.

Recreate a classic game

I love old arcade, Nintendo, and Sega games. I am really stuck in that 8-bit retro world and always look back to the games I played as a child to find inspiration. One of the first games I ever built in Flash 4 was Duck Hunt. Recently, I built a clone of Frogger. After building Frogger, I re-skinned it and put my own spin on it. Don't underestimate the importance of simply trying to recreate an existing game that works well, then modifying it with your own take or changing the game system to create a new game. If you look back through the history of video games, you will see a natural evolution of one game picking up or modifying another game's mechanics. Just make sure you give credit where credit is due and don't blatantly go out and steal another person or company's game.

Do a daily code warmup

A big part of my development routine is doing 30-minute code warmups. This is actually a technique I picked up when I was a fine artist and my mentor used to make me do 30 minutes of sketching before I started painting. Doing a small experiment or trying to solve a development problem can really get your brain going and help you be way more creative when you finally sit down to code your own game.

Experiment

Finally, this should go without saying, experiment as much as possible. This goes hand in hand with the daily code warmup. I like to pick game systems or interesting gameplay concepts, then try to reproduce them or make them better. Take a simple turn-based combat system or an inventory system, for example, and just try to code one from scratch. As you build out more of these experiments and game system studies, you can quickly begin to put them together to help you prototype out game ideas even quicker.

Books to Read

There are a lot of really good books on game development, so I thought I would highlight the three most important ones I feel are must-reads for any aspiring game developer:

"A Theory of Fun for Game Design" by Raph Koster

This is a great book that attempts to answer the question "What is fun?" and more importantly "What is a game?" It's an easy read with absolutely no code and all theory.

"Level Up!: The Guide to Great Video Game Design" by Scott Rogers

If you are interested in understanding the technical side of game design as in how to build a game design document, pitching games, and more practice than theory then this is the book to read. Again, this book doesn't have any code in it, but the lessons you will learn will help make you a much better game designer.

"Rules of Play: Game Design Fundamentals" by Katie Salen and Eric Zimmerman

If you ever took a course on game design, then this would be your required reading. The book approaches the question of game design from a very academic point of view. The book is long, detailed, and full of homework-type examples to practice your skills. This book is for the serious game designer looking to not only master the art of game design but to be able to speak about it on a higher level.

CHAPTER 4

Building A Game

In the following chapter, we are going to build a game called **Resident Raver**, in which the player controls an unnamed hero who is trying to escape a college dorm overrun by raver zombies. The hero has several weapons at his disposal to help him escape, while also navigating platform-based obstacles. I have gone ahead and created all the assets you will need for the final game.

Before moving onto the next section, make sure you copy over the contents of the media folder that is included in the book's example files folder. This will contain all the assets you will need for the rest of the book. In it you will find sprites, map tiles, and sounds.

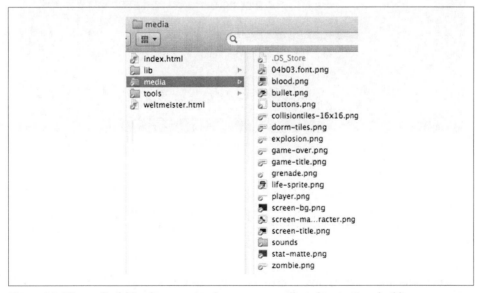

Figure 4-1. The media folder that contains the assets you will need to continue building your game.

It's okay to replace the default media directory with the one we will be using for this book.

Creating Our First Level

Now that we have learned about creating graphics for our game, we can start building our first level. Let's open up Weltmeister and create a simple level. When you open up Weltmeister for the first time, you will see that an untitled.js file has been created for you, but that the level is empty. Before we can even start creating our level, we will need to add our map tile sprite sheet. Create a new layer and call it main. This is where we will start drawing our level. You can create this new layer by clicking the plus icon on the top right of the screen next to the Layers label.

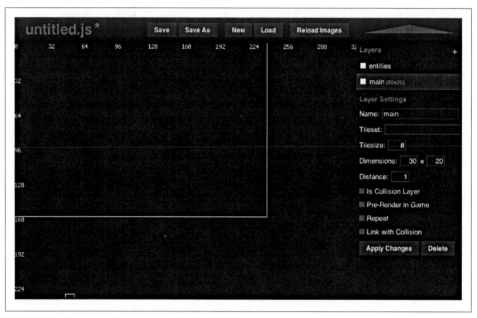

Figure 4-2. This is what you will see after creating your new layer.

When a new layer is created, its bounding box will be displayed showing the borders of the layer. You can't draw tiles outside of this box. This is based on the layer's dimensions, which are configured as part of the layer's properties. Here is a summary of what each property represents:

Name
   This is the name of the layer. It can be anything you want.

Tileset
   This is the path to the Tileset image file you want to use for this layer. Clicking on this property will bring up a list of directories in your project file.

Tilesize

This represents the size of each tile in your sprite sheet. By default, it is set to 8.

Dimensions

This represents how large the layer is. By default, it is set to 30×30 tiles. Since tiles are set to 8 pixels by default, this layer is 240×160 pixels.

Distance

This is the distance from the camera, similar to Z index in HTML. This is useful for background layers you want to scroll at a different speed than the foreground layers to create a parallax scrolling effect.

Is Collision Layer

This toggle allows you to use the layer for collision detection, which we will cover later on.

Pre-Render In Game

This will pre-render your map, which can help increase the performance of your game, especially on mobile devices, but you will not be able to have animated tiles.

Repeat

This is also a background layer property that allows you to repeat your layer when it scrolls by in the background. Think of this more as a texture that is repeated inside of the layer.

Now we are ready to make our first level. Let's click on the Tileset field and select our map tiles. After clicking on the Tileset input field, you should see the root directory of your project from a drop-down menu, as seen in Figure 4-3. Select media, and there you can select `dorm-tiles.png`. You will also need to set the Tilesize to 16. Make sure to apply the changes so your selections are saved.

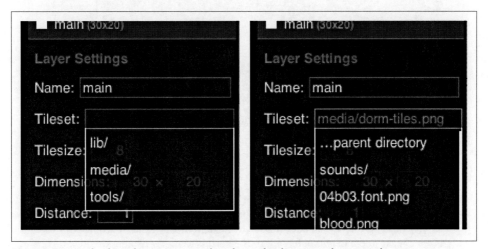

Figure 4-3. Use the drop-down menu to select the media directory where our tile sprites are.

Now, click inside the map editor and press the space bar to bring up the tile painter (Figure 4-4).

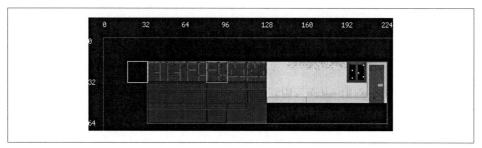

Figure 4-4. All the tiles you can paint your level with.

The tile painter is very easy to use. While your tile set is visible, simply select the tile you want to use by clicking it with your mouse. The tile set will disappear and you will now be able to place your selected tile by clicking anywhere in the layer. You can also click and drag to create many tiles of the same artwork. When you want to change tiles, press the space bar again, select a new tile, and resume clicking to place the new tiles.

Notice the yellow box at the beginning of your sprite sheet that looks empty? Selecting this allows you to erase tiles you have already painted. Weltmeister automatically creates the empty tile for you so you don't need to add it to your sprite sheet. Let's draw the foundation of our level, shown in Figure 4-5.

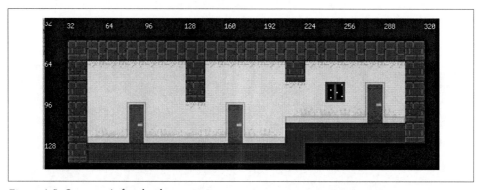

Figure 4-5. Our game's first level.

 When you start creating your own level, feel free to experiment with the tiles and add some variety to your textures. You don't have to follow this example 100%, but I wanted to create something that was quick to make and had two different ground heights to it. It's also important to note that I never start my maps at exactly 0,0, in case I need more space at the top of the lefthand side later on.

I know this level doesn't look very exciting yet but, don't worry, we will get into more complex level creation later on.

Saving/Loading Maps in Weltmeister

Save your map by hitting Save at the top of the editor. You will notice that, by default, Weltmeister wants to put levels in the lib/game/levels/ directory. This is very important, because this is where Impact will automatically look for your game's levels. Later on, we will be able to simply tell Impact to load your level by name instead of having to pass it the full directory path.

Figure 4-6. Levels are automatically saved inside the game's levels directory.

Let's name our level dorm1.js. Note that we have to add the .js file extension to our level. The level file is actually a JSON file. The editor will give you an error if you forget to add the correct extension.

 It's important to note that you will need to have PHP set up in order to save. The editor itself is built with JavaScript, but the save API uses PHP. This should be handled automatically if you're using the recommended MAMP or XAMP applications discussed in Chapter 1.

You can also easily load any level you have created by selecting Load from the top menu.

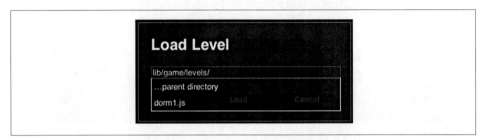

Figure 4-7. It is easy to load any level you have already created.

You will see a list of all the maps you have created. By default, Weltmeister automatically attempts to load the last level you were working in.

CollisionMaps

Now that we have our level's tiles in place we need to set up a collision layer. This tells Impact what tiles are passable and impassable to the game's entities. To set this up, we need to create a new layer called `collision` and set the Tilesize to 16. Now, you can select `Is Collision Layer` from the layer options, and a default set of collision tiles will automatically be loaded for you. Once you have the collision layer in place, let's start painting.

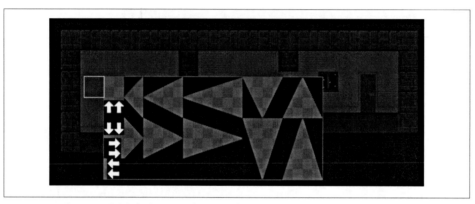

Figure 4-8. These are the default sprites for the collision tiles.

As seen in Figure 4-8, there are a lot of different collision tiles for us to choose from. Most of these tiles help support collisions with slopes. We are going to focus on the first solid tile, which is the pink square in the upper-left corner. Let's paint on top of our main level's walls.

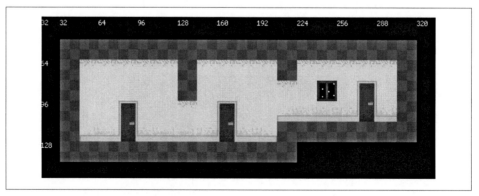

Figure 4-9. Our level with the collision tiles in place.

Usually, I put the collision layer underneath the main layer. You can reorder layers at any time by simply dragging them around. Now, when we create our player and monsters, Impact will make sure they don't fall through the floor.

It looks like we are finally ready to start building our game!

The Main Class

When setting up a new Impact project from the template project, you will see a `main.js` file in your game directory. The main class is the entry point to your application and will contain some of the core logic, such as binding keyboard events and logic for making the camera follow the player. Most importantly, the main file also defines and loads any required files or global functions in your game. Here is the default `main.js` class you will start with:

```
1    ig.module(
2        'game.main'
3    )
4    .requires(
5        'impact.game',
6        'impact.font'
7    )
8    .defines(function(){
9
10       MyGame = ig.Game.extend({
11
12           // Load a font
13           font: new ig.Font( 'media/04b03.font.png' ),
14
15
16           init: function() {
17               // Initialize your game here; bind keys etc.
18           },
19
20           update: function() {
21               // Update all entities and backgroundMaps
22               this.parent();
23
24               // Add your own, additional update code here
25           },
26
27           draw: function() {
28               // Draw all entities and backgroundMaps
29               this.parent();
30
31
32               // Add your own drawing code here
33               var x = ig.system.width/2,
34               y = ig.system.height/2;
35
36               this.font.draw( 'It Works!', x, y, ig.Font.ALIGN.CENTER );
37           }
```

```
38          });
39
40
41          });
42
43
44      // Start the Game with 60fps, a resolution of 320×240, scaled
45          // up by a factor of 2
46          ig.main( '#canvas', MyGame, 60, 320, 240, 2 );
47
48      });
49
```

Let's take a moment to go through some of the high-level code.

```
ig.module(
    'game.main'
)
```

The above code represents the namespace of your game. As you can see, this also defines the name of your main class.

```
.requires(
    'impact.game',
    'impact.font'
)
```

The first block of code above defines the class name and, as a result, file name of the module. The second block specifies which classes are needed by the game. Our main class will inherit from the Game class, and the Font class will be used to instantiate a font we'll use for onscreen text display. These classes will automatically load when your game is run for the first time.

Next, everything in the .defines(function(){ ... }) block of code is your game logic. As you can see, Game is extended as described, and the Font class is used to populate a property called font with the font class and its font sprite sheet:

```
.defines(function(){

    MyGame = ig.Game.extend({

            // Load a font
            font: new ig.Font( 'media/04b03.font.png' ),
```

Then, we define some scaffolding code for init(), update(), and draw(). The draw() method is the only one with executable code in it. The default class needs to re-render the font on each draw call, so this default code simply gets the x,y position of where the text field should go, so the engine knows where to draw the font graphic.

Before moving on, there is one more thing that is important to highlight from the last few lines of the `main.js` file:

```
// Start the Game with 60fps, a resolution of 320×240, scaled
// up by a factor of 2
ig.main( '#canvas', MyGame, 60, 320, 240, 2 );
});
```

This is the code that initializes your game. As you can see, we pass the ID of the Canvas element to our game's constructor, a name for our game instance, and the frame rate and size into the `ig.main` constructor. The last value of 2 represents the scale of your game. This will upscale all of your game's graphics by 2.

Customizing the Main Class

To get started, let's delete the font code from the draw method, but make sure you leave `this.parent()`. We can also now delete the font variable from the beginning of the class.

Now with the "It Works!" text removed, the first thing we want our game to do when it starts is load the level we just created. Change the `.requires(...)` block to load the level:

```
.requires(
    'impact.game',
    'game.levels.dorm1'
)
```

Unfortunately, if you refresh your game, nothing is going to display. We will need to tell the game to load our level. Add the following code to your `init()` method:

```
init: function() {
    this.loadLevel( LevelDorm1 );
},
```

Now, refresh your game.

Key Binding

Impact has an easy-to-use input class, ideal for capturing keyboard input, which can be found in the `ig.input` namespace. To capture keyboard events, we will need to bind the key press event to the desired key in the input class. Let's put the following code at the beginning of the `init()` function in `main.js`, just above our load level code:

```
// Bind keys
ig.input.bind( ig.KEY.LEFT_ARROW, 'left' );
ig.input.bind( ig.KEY.RIGHT_ARROW, 'right' );
ig.input.bind( ig.KEY.X, 'jump' );
ig.input.bind( ig.KEY.C, 'shoot' );
```

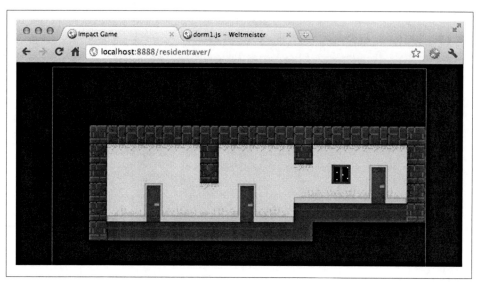

Figure 4-10. The level loaded when the game is refreshed.

For our game, we are going to track the left and right arrows along with the X and C keys. This is the first step in setting up controls for your game. In a little while, we'll set up code to react to the left, right, jump and shoot commands those keys will trigger.

There is a list of constants that contains all the keys Impact can use in the `ig.KEY` class. To use them, simply apply a custom label to a key so that when we poll for input during game play, we will be able to react to the desired event when each key is pressed.

Creating the Player Class

The player will be the first entity we build for our game. Entities are anything that exist in the level that are not part of the map. Monsters, bullets, doors, triggers, etc., are all considered entities. Our player class will extend the core `entity.js` class so it can inherit some basic behavior to get us started. Let's begin by creating a new `player.js` file in the `lib/game/entities` directory.

Now, add the following code to our file:

```
1   ig.module(
2       'game.entities.player'
3   )
4   .requires(
5       'impact.entity'
6   )
7   .defines(function(){
8       EntityPlayer = ig.Entity.extend({
9
10      });
11  });
```

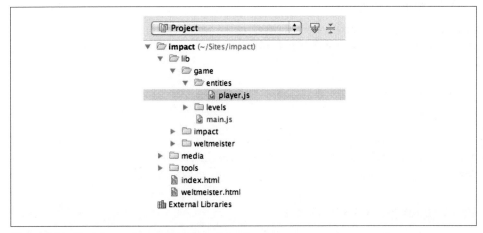

Figure 4-11. Our player class goes in the entities directory.

This is the basic structure for creating entities in Impact. As discussed previously, we define the module name and reference any required classes, then define the class itself, extending `ig.Entity`. At this point, however, nothing will happen if you refresh your game. We still need to set up the player and add it to the level. To do that, let's add some properties to this class.

Using Your Sprite Sheet

Start by setting up an animation sheet. Add the following to the `EntityPlayer` code block:

```
EntityPlayer = ig.Entity.extend({
    animSheet: new ig.AnimationSheet( 'media/player.png', 16, 16 ),
});
```

This tells our player that it will use `player.png` in the media folder and that its tiles are 16×16. We are also going to need to define some values for the size and offset of the player. We'll add the following underneath where we set up our animation sheet:

```
size: {x: 8, y:14},
offset: {x: 4, y: 2},
flip: false,
```

The `size` property represents the actual size of the player. The `offset` property describes any change in the player size needed to make collisions more accurate. In this case, we're offsetting the bounding box used for collisions by 4 pixels on the left and right, and 2 pixels on top and bottom. By making the collision area smaller than the sprite, we can better account for the transparent space around the graphic. Finally, we don't flip the player, so it remains oriented in its original direction.

Adding Simple Physics

Next let's set up some physics properties, such as velocity, friction, rate of acceleration in the ground and air, and jump strength.

```
maxVel: {x: 100, y: 150},
friction: {x: 600, y: 0},
accelGround: 400,
accelAir: 200,
jump: 200,
```

These properties define how our player can move in the environment. Impact handles all of the physics calculations for us. Once we get the player up and running, you should feel free to tweak these values to see how they affect your game.

Defining Animation Sequences

With the player's core values out of the way, we can look into setting up animation sequences. Create an init() method underneath where we defined the properties in the player class and add the following code to it:

```
init: function( x, y, settings ) {
    this.parent( x, y, settings );
    this.addAnim( 'idle', 1, [0] );
    this.addAnim( 'run', 0.07, [0,1,2,3,4,5] );
    this.addAnim( 'jump', 1, [9] );
    this.addAnim( 'fall', 0.4, [6,7] );
},
```

This function passes the x,y and settings values up to the parent's init() method. This is very important, since entities need to know their starting x,y positions and any settings assigned to them when being created in the level. You can also pass in additional values through the level editor, which get attached to the settings object during the construction of the entities.

As discussed earlier, it's easy to set up animations. Use the entity class's addAnim() method and pass it an ID (or name) for the animation, along with the duration and an array for the frames from the sprite sheet. Before we move on, let's make sure your player class looks like this:

```
1    ig.module(
2        'game.entities.player'
3    )
4    .requires(
5        'impact.entity'
6    )
7    .defines(function(){
8        EntityPlayer = ig.Entity.extend({
9            animSheet: new ig.AnimationSheet( 'media/player.png', 16, 16 ),
10           size: {x: 8, y:14},
11           offset: {x: 4, y: 2},
12           flip: false,
```

```
13          maxVel: {x: 100, y: 150},
14          friction: {x: 600, y: 0},
15          accelGround: 400,
16          accelAir: 200,
17          jump: 200,
18          init: function( x, y, settings ) {
19              this.parent( x, y, settings );
20              // Add the animations
21              this.addAnim( 'idle', 1, [0] );
22              this.addAnim( 'run', 0.07, [0,1,2,3,4,5] );
23              this.addAnim( 'jump', 1, [9] );
24              this.addAnim( 'fall', 0.4, [6,7] );
25          }
26      });
27  });
```

At this point, we are ready to switch back over to Weltmeister and add our player. When you load the editor back up, you should see our dorm1.js level. If it's not there, simply load it up manually. When you load the level, the entities layer should automatically be highlighted. This layer works just like the other layers we created, so move over to the Canvas area and press the space bar to see the list of entities you can add to the level. Right now, you should see the player from the drop-down menu.

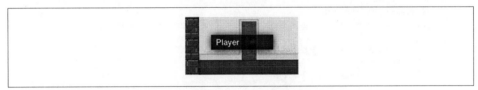

Figure 4-12. Select the player from the pop-up entity menu.

Select the player and add him to the level. You can place him anywhere for now; I put mine on the far left of the level. Also, make sure you hit Save once you are happy with your player's start position.

Figure 4-13. A preview of the player in the level editor.

It's also important to note that as of version 1.19 of Impact, you no longer need to add each entity to your game's requires block; it is now automatically handled for you when the level is loaded. Now you are ready to test out your game. Go to your browser and hit refresh.

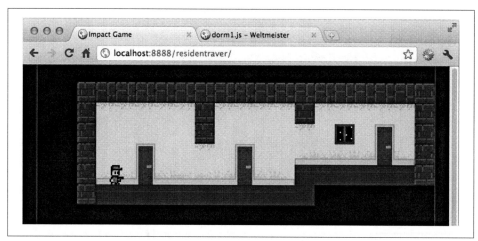

Figure 4-14. The player is now in our game's level.

You should now see your player in the game, but you will not be able to move him. Let's fix that. Go back into the player.js class and add the following update() function:

```
update: function() {
    // move left or right
    var accel = this.standing ? this.accelGround : this.accelAir;
    if( ig.input.state('left') ) {
        this.accel.x = -accel;
        this.flip = true;
    }else if( ig.input.state('right') ) {
        this.accel.x = accel;
        this.flip = false;
    }else{
        this.accel.x = 0;
    }
    // jump
    if( this.standing && ig.input.pressed('jump') ) {
        this.vel.y = -this.jump;
    }
    // move!
    this.parent();
},
```

As you continue adding code to your game, always make sure there is a comma to separate new functions, or you may get an error when you try to preview your code.

Now, you are ready to refresh the game and test out moving the player. As you can see, we can move our player, but he doesn't animate or fall off ledges. We are going to need to set the gravity of the game. We can do this in main.js. Add the following property to that class:

```
MyGame = ig.Game.extend({
    gravity: 300,
    init: function() {
```

Now, if you go back to your game, you will be able to jump and fall off ledges. When you test it out, though, you will not have a clean-looking fall animation. Let's add in some additional code to keep track of the player's velocity in order to show the correct animation such as jump, fall, idle, and run. This should go below our jump code in the `player.js` class:

```
// set the current animation, based on the player's speed
if( this.vel.y < 0 ) {
    this.currentAnim = this.anims.jump;
}else if( this.vel.y > 0 ) {
    this.currentAnim = this.anims.fall;
}else if( this.vel.x != 0 ) {
    this.currentAnim = this.anims.run;
}else{
    this.currentAnim = this.anims.idle;
}
```

Now, we should be able to jump and run with corresponding animation, but there is one thing missing. We need a way to tell the player to flip his animation based on the direction he is running. We can do this by adding the following code just before the `this.parent()` call in the `player.js` update function:

```
this.currentAnim.flip.x = this.flip;
```

Now we have a fully functional player. Let's give it one more test and make sure everything works. At this point, our level is kind of boring—so let's add a few monsters to the game.

Creating a Monster Class

Creating a monster is similar to creating a player. In fact, we are going to use the same basic class code but change its name and namespace. Create a new file called `zombie.js` in the entities folder.

Now, copy the following code into the monster class:

```
1    ig.module(
2        'game.entities.zombie'
3    )
4    .requires(
5        'impact.entity'
6    )
7    .defines(function(){
8        EntityZombie = ig.Entity.extend({
9
10        });
11    });
```

As you can see, we simply changed the entity name and class name, but everything else is the same as the code we used to start the player class. Now we are ready to add our monster's animation and set its initial properties:

```
animSheet: new ig.AnimationSheet( 'media/zombie.png', 16, 16 ),
size: {x: 8, y:14},
offset: {x: 4, y: 2},
maxVel: {x: 100, y: 100},
flip: false,
```

Now we need to set up the animations just like we did for the player. This is a simple monster, so there are only a few sprites representing its animation. Let's create a new init() method with the following code:

```
init: function( x, y, settings ) {
    this.parent( x, y, settings );
    this.addAnim('walk', .07, [0,1,2,3,4,5]);
},
```

With our default animation in place, we can start adding instances of the monster to test the level. Let's switch over to Weltmeister, select the entities layer, and then add a monster by clicking into the layer and pressing the space bar, just as we did when adding the player. You can then click on the map to add the monster where you want it.

Figure 4-15. Select Zombie from the drop-down entity list.

Feel free to add a few of them, as shown in Figure 4-16.

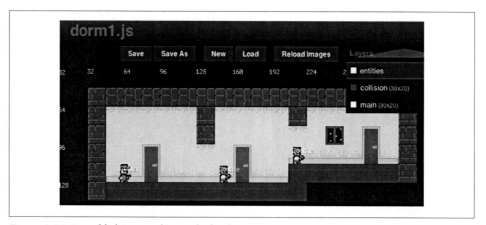

Figure 4-16. I've added two zombies to the level.

Once you have done this, refresh the game in your browser and you should see your new monsters. We haven't added any movement logic yet, so they don't do much right now. Let's add some basic code to make them walk back and forth, but be smart enough not to fall off ledges. We'll need to create an update function that will handle the basic movement logic or AI (Artificial Intelligence) for our monster:

```
update: function() {
    // near an edge? return!
    if( !ig.game.collisionMap.getTile(
            this.pos.x + (this.flip ? +4 : this.size.x -4),
                this.pos.y + this.size.y+1
            )
    ) {
            this.flip = !this.flip;
    }
    var xdir = this.flip ? -1 : 1;
    this.vel.x = this.speed * xdir;
    this.currentAnim.flip.x = this.flip;
    this.parent();
},
```

This function tests to see if the monster hits anything in the collision map. If it does, we toggle the value of the class flip property. After testing, the direction and velocity are updated before this.parent() is called. We will also need to define the monster's friction and speed. You can add that toward the top of the class just under where we define the flip property:

```
friction: {x: 150, y: 0},
speed: 14,
```

Refresh the game to take a look at it in action. You will see the monster instances moving around, and when they hit the edge of a ledge, they flip and go the other way.

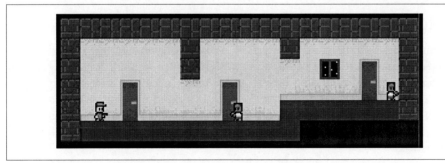

Figure 4-17. We want to make sure our zombies flip direction once they hit a wall or the end of a platform.

We just need to add a few more lines of code to clean this up. Add the following block of code to the end of your defines() function:

```
handleMovementTrace: function( res ) {
    this.parent( res );
```

```
        // collision with a wall? return!
        if( res.collision.x ) {
            this.flip = !this.flip;
        }
    },
```

This helps make sure that if a monster runs into a wall, that it also turns around. Collisions with walls and the collision map are handled through the `handleMovement Trace` function. Now we have covered all our bases and made sure our zombies will not fall off ledges or platforms, but we still have one issue. There is no collision detection between the monster and the player.

Figure 4-18. The player simply passes through zombies without collision detection.

Before we get into adding more code to the monster, we need to talk a little bit about entity-based collision detection in Impact.

So far, we've handled simple interactions with walls and platforms manually. However, Impact has built-in collision detection that we can use for interaction between our entities. That is, we can focus on setting up collision relationships instead of creating all that collision code from scratch. Let's look a little closer at how we can use Impact to do this work for us.

Collision Detection

Since Impact has built-in collision detection, we can focus on setting up collision relationships instead of creating all the necessary code from scratch. Impact's collision detection is based on bounding boxes. A bounding box is an imaginary rectangle around a sprite. If a sprite is 16×16 pixels, the box around it would be the same size. During a bounding box collision text, two entity's boxes are overlapping. This kind of collision detection is incredibly fast and covers a good portion of the use cases you will probably need.

 It is important to note that one of the issues with bounding box collision is that it doesn't take into account any transparent space around your sprite. This is why we had to tweak the `size` and `offset` values of our entities to help make our collision look as clean as possible.

Let's take a look at how we can add collision detection to entities in our game.

type Property

The .type property allows us to group entities when doing collision detection. For example, you might assign all friendly entities to one group, and all enemy entities to another group. This way, you can set up your file so neither group will collide with their own types, but friendlies will collide with enemies, and vice versa. There are three .types in Impact that you can reference using their constant values:

```
ig.Entity.TYPE.NONE
ig.Entity.TYPE.A
ig.Entity.TYPE.B
```

By default, all entities are set to NONE. The other two groups are left open for your own needs. So, for instance, you can set all friendly entities to TYPE.A and hostile entities will check for collisions with TYPE.A only.

checkAgainst Property

The .checkAgainst property tells an entity which type property to check for when it collides with another entity. An entity can check for four types during the collision:

```
ig.Entity.TYPE.NONE
ig.Entity.TYPE.A
ig.Entity.TYPE.B
ig.Entity.TYPE.BOTH
```

The default value is always set to NONE. When two entities overlap, the .checkAgainst property of one entity is compared with the .type property of the other. If there is a match, the first entity's check() method is called, and the latter object with which it collided is sent to the method as a parameter. You can customize the check() method to respond to such a collision

This example, which we'll discuss in greater detail in a moment, shows damage applied after such a collision:

```
check: function( other ) {
    other.receiveDamage( 10, this );
}
```

collides Property

The final part of collision detection we need to learn about is the .collides property. This property determines how the entity collides with other entities. It's important to note that this is independent of the collision map. This is strictly an entity-to-entity collision event. There are several types of collision property values:

```
ig.Entity.COLLIDES.NEVER
ig.Entity.COLLIDES.LITE
ig.Entity.COLLIDES.PASSIVE
```

```
ig.Entity.COLLIDES.ACTIVE
ig.Entity.COLLIDES.FIXED
```

By default, the `collides` property is set to `NEVER`, which ignores all collisions. `FIXED` is used for objects such as walls and platforms that won't move *as a result of a collision*. It's important to note that entities with a `FIXED` `collides` property may still move, just not when colliding with another entity. Elevators and moving platforms are good examples of this situation.

The remaining three `collides` values determine which entities move after a collision. If two `ACTIVE` entities collide, they will both move apart. The same is true when `ACTIVE` and `PASSIVE` entities collide, but the `PASSIVE` collides value exists so that entities of similar types can overlap without causing a resulting movement. So, when a `PASSIVE` entity collides with another `PASSIVE` entity, neither is moved by the collision.

Finally, where `FIXED` describes a "strong" entity that never moves away from a collision, `LITE` is used to specify a "weak" entity—one which always moves away from a collision.

Now that we have covered the collision properties entities have, let's start setting up our own player and monster to have collision detection. Open up the `player.js` class and add the following properties:

```
type: ig.Entity.TYPE.A,
checkAgainst: ig.Entity.TYPE.NONE,
collides: ig.Entity.COLLIDES.PASSIVE,
```

Here, we are setting up all three collision properties for the player. We assign the player to `TYPE.A`, which will represent our friendly group. Next, we'll set `.checkAgainst` to `NONE`. In our example, we'll let the monster handle the collisions and, as shown in the previous section, apply damage to the player. Finally, we'll set `.collides` to `PASSIVE`. This will prevent overlaps with another `PASSIVE` entity moving either entity as a result of the collision.

Now it's time to set up our monster. Open up the `zombie.js` class and add the following:

```
type: ig.Entity.TYPE.B,
checkAgainst: ig.Entity.TYPE.A,
collides: ig.Entity.COLLIDES.PASSIVE,
```

We are setting our monster to the enemy group, which is `TYPE.B`. Since the player belongs to group `TYPE.A`, we will check against that group for collisions. And finally, we also set the enemy `.collides` property to `PASSIVE`. This will allow us to react when a collision is detected with the player, but because both entity `.collides` properties are set to `PASSIVE`, Impact won't automatically move either of the players due to the collision.

If you tested your game now, it would appear that no collisions occur. This is because we set the collides property for all entities to PASSIVE, and Impact won't adjust the position of either entity after a collision. We need to add some more code in the monster class to handle the collision when it is detected. Add the following method to the `zombie.js` class:

```
check: function( other ) {
    other.receiveDamage( 10, this );
}
```

You may recall during the discussion of the .checkAgainst property that this code applies damage to the entity the monster collides with. Remember that the colliding entity is passed to the function as an argument (other). This code executes Impact's built-in receiveDamage() method in the player entity, and passes a value of 10, as well as a reference to the monster, to the player. The end result is that the player will lose all his health (10 points, by default).

Now, if you test the game, when the player hits a monster, he should be immediately killed. Visually, the player just disappears, since we haven't created a death animation.

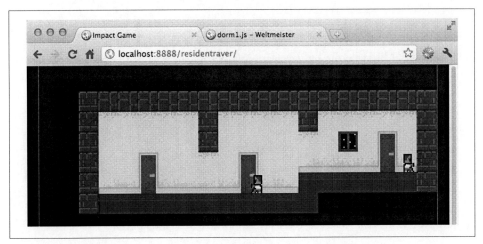

Figure 4-19. The player is removed from the screen once the zombie kills him.

Next, we will discuss health.

Health

Each entity has a health property. By default, this is set to 10. This value is incredibly useful if you are taking advantage of the built-in receiveDamage() method to subtract an entity's health. To change an entity's initial health, you can simply set this value in your class's properties like so:

```
health: 20,
```

If we applied this to our player now, there would be no apparent change. Multiple collisions occur when passive entities overlap, because Impact doesn't automatically resolve their positions and push the weaker entity away. In the next section, we'll introduce weapons, and later you can tweak this value in the monster class to get a better result. For now we can just leave it as is.

Weapons

Right now, our player is defenseless. As soon as he hits a monster, he dies, and there is no way for the player to kill a monster. Well, that is about to change. One way to add a weapon is to create a new entity class. Weltmeister will then offer it as an option when placing entities on the map—convenient if you want to place weapons the player can pick up during the game. However, if your player will have access to the weapon throughout the game, you can keep Weltmeister's menu options simple by creating an inner class within the `player.js` file.

Let's find the player class's closing blocks around line 59. Between the two closing block tags is where we will put our inner class:

```
EntityBullet = ig.Entity.extend({

});
```

Now you should have your bullet entity just before the end of the `player.js` class as shown in Figure 4-20.

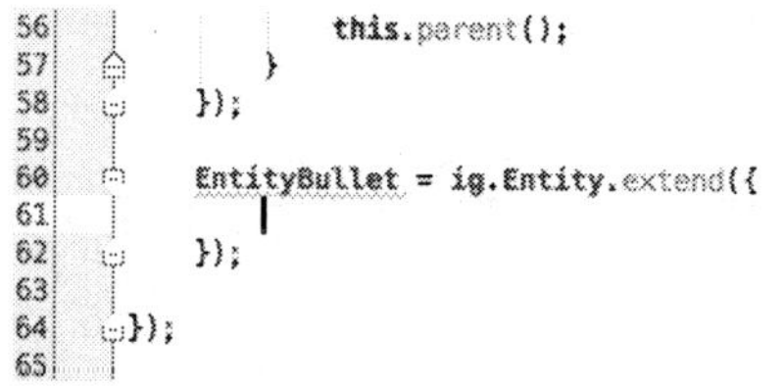

Figure 4-20. Add the EntityBullet class just before the end of the player module.

Now we are ready to customize our player's weapon.

As you can see, our `EntityBullet` is just like any other entity you have created. It extends `ig.Entity`, which means it has all the same inherited properties and methods as our player and monster. Basically, we are going to spawn a new bullet every time the player presses the fire button and, based on which way the player is facing, the bullet entity will move in that direction. When the bullet hits a wall or monster, it will remove itself and, in the case of a monster, apply damage. Let's start by adding a few properties to our bullet:

```
size: {x: 5, y: 3},
animSheet: new ig.AnimationSheet( 'media/bullet.png', 5, 3 ),
maxVel: {x: 200, y: 0},
```

This will set up our bullet's size, graphic, and maximum velocity. It's important to note that our bullets don't have y velocity since they only move horizontally. Also, we need to make sure our bullet can move faster than the player. We don't want to fire our gun and run into or beyond our bullet as it flies through the air. Next, we will need to set up some collision information for the bullet:

```
type: ig.Entity.TYPE.NONE,
checkAgainst: ig.Entity.TYPE.B,
collides: ig.Entity.COLLIDES.PASSIVE,
```

As you can see, we are going to have our bullet test for TYPE.B entities, and its collides property is set to passive so it doesn't displace entities it collides with. Now we can add our init() method:

```
init: function( x, y, settings ) {
    this.parent( x + (settings.flip ? -4 : 8) , y+8, settings );
    this.vel.x = this.accel.x = (settings.flip ? -this.maxVel.x : this.maxVel.x);
    this.addAnim( 'idle', 0.2, [0] );
},
```

Here we are taking the flip value that will be passed into the EntityBullet via the optional settings object and applying an offset to the x,y values we pass to the parent method. This ensures that the bullet starts in the correct position and appears to be fired from the gun. Next, we set the velocity and acceleration x value to our maximum velocity x value. If the player is facing left, make this negative. This forces the bullet to fire at its maximum speed instead of slowly accelerating toward its maximum velocity.

Now we need to test for our collisions. Let's start by reacting any time the bullet hits something in the collision layer:

```
handleMovementTrace: function( res ) {
    this.parent( res );
    if( res.collision.x || res.collision.y ){
        this.kill();
    }
},
```

The handleMovementTrace() gets called while an entity is moving. This method is associated with the collision map, so we can detect when an entity hits a wall. We check the res object parameter if a collision happens on the x or y values.

```
check: function( other ) {
    other.receiveDamage( 3, this );
    this.kill();
}
```

All we need to do now is add some code to our player in order to fire the bullets.

Firing the Weapon

Since inner classes are just like any other class we would create in Impact, we can simply use the ig.game built-in spawnEntity() method to create a new instance of the bullet when the player presses the fire key. Our player and monster are created during the level parsing process, so we have not had to manually instantiate an entity yet. The spawnEntity() function helps ensure that when we create a new entity, it gets added to Impact's render list. Open up your player.js class and put the following code under the jump logic in the update method:

```
// shoot
if( ig.input.pressed('shoot') ) {
    ig.game.spawnEntity( EntityBullet, this.pos.x, this.pos.y, {flip:this.flip} );
}
```

As you can see, we are going to look for the shoot event, which we bound to the C key in our main class. This should be very straightforward—we tell ig.game that we are going to spawn a new entity. The spawnEntity() method needs a reference to the class we want to create and its starting x,y position, along with any additional settings we want to pass to the new entity. Notice here that we create a generic object with a property called flip with the player's flip value. This is what tells the bullet which direction it should be fired.

At this point, we can test that our gun works by refreshing the game in the browser and hitting C. So, now you should be able to fire your weapon and kill the monsters.

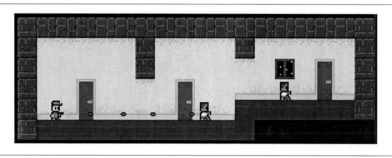

Figure 4-21. You should see bullets being fired when you press the C key.

At this point, the monsters will die after a few shots. If you change the monsters' life property to something lower, it will take less shots to kill them. This is because on every collision the bullet detects with an enemy, it calls receivedDamage() and passes in 3 as the value. Likewise, you can make the bullets stronger by changing the amount of damage they apply.

Right now, our gun is kind of boring. Let's add another weapon to the mix and see what happens.

Add Multiple Weapons

So, we built a basic gun that fires bullets, but what about adding something a little more exciting? How about a grenade that bounces and explodes when it hits stuff? We can easily add in new types of weapons just like we did with our bullet. Let's set up the beginning of our grenade class after our EntityBullet. Add the following inner class to your player.js module:

```
EntityGrenade = ig.Entity.extend({

});
```

Just like with our bullet, we are ready to customize the grenade's properties. We will need to give it a graphic and set the size and offset:

```
size: {x: 4, y: 4},
offset: {x: 2, y: 2},
animSheet: new ig.AnimationSheet( 'media/grenade.png', 8, 8 ),
```

Now let's set up our collision detection:

```
type: ig.Entity.TYPE.NONE,
checkAgainst: ig.Entity.TYPE.BOTH,
collides: ig.Entity.COLLIDES.PASSIVE,
```

Pay special attention to the fact that we are setting checkAgainst to TYPE.BOTH. What this means is that our grenade can collide with our zombie and our player. You'll see how this works when we are ready to test our grenade later on. However, in order for our grenade to move and bounce, we will need to add a few additional properties. Add the following to your grenade class:

```
maxVel: {x: 200, y: 200},
bounciness: 0.6,
bounceCounter: 0,
```

Here, we are setting our grenade's maximum velocity. Also, we are going to keep track of how many times it will bounce before blowing up, as well as its bounciness value. You can tweak these values once we enable the player to actually fire the grenade, so you can test what effect the bounciness value will have.

Let's override the init() method with the following code:

```
init: function( x, y, settings ) {
    this.parent( x + (settings.flip ? -4 : 7), y, settings );
    this.vel.x = (settings.flip ? -this.maxVel.x : this.maxVel.x);
    this.vel.y = -(50 + (Math.random()*100));
    this.addAnim( 'idle', 0.2, [0,1] );
},
```

Here, we are going to determine the beginning x velocity based on a flip parameter that will be passed in via the settings object. Just like with our bullet, when the player fires the grenade we will set the player's own flip value into a property of the settings object so that we know what direction to fire the grenade. It's also incredibly important that we get the start x,y position offset correct. Since the grenade can collide with the player, we wouldn't want it to fire the weapon and instantly blow up.

Next, we offset the y velocity by negative 50 plus a random number that ranges from 0 to 100, which will help add an arc to the grenade when it gets fired. The randomness makes sure that the player throws the grenade slightly differently each time. This, along with the fact that the grenade can also kill the player, will help balance the fact that this is a more powerful weapon. After that, we just set the idle animation to display sprites 0 and 1, which will loop through images of the grenade rotating as it flies through the air.

We are getting very close to testing out our grenade, but before we do, we'll have to override the handleMovementTrace() method and write some logic to handle collisions, track the number of bounces, and remove the grenade from the display if it bounces too many times:

```
handleMovementTrace: function( res ) {
    this.parent( res );
    if( res.collision.x || res.collision.y ) {
        // only bounce 3 times
        this.bounceCounter++;
        if( this.bounceCounter > 3 ) {
            this.kill();
        }
    }
},
```

This works exactly like our bullet, except that when a collision is detected, we increment the .bounceCounter by 1. If the .bounceCounter is greater than 3, we kill the grenade. We will talk more about the entity's kill() method later.

Now that we can handle tracking bounces, let's add logic when the grenade collides with an enemy. Like we did before in the EntityBullet class, we are going to override the check function, which gets called when a .checkAgainst group has been detected. Add the following function to your grenade class:

```
check: function( other ) {
    other.receiveDamage( 10, this );
    this.kill();
}
```

Finally, we have increased the damage of the grenade so that it kills anything in a single hit. Now, all we need to do in order to have the player toggle between weapons is bind a new key to toggle between the weapons and then have the player swap between the correct one. Let's add the following bind logic into our main.js init() function:

```
ig.input.bind( ig.KEY.TAB, 'switch' );
```

Now, if we go back into our player class, we will need a way to keep track of the current weapon. Add the following property to the beginning of our EntityPlayer class in the player.js file:

```
weapon: 0,
totalWeapons: 2,
```

From there, we can add a simple test to see when the player presses the weapon toggle button, so we can toggle the weapon property. Add the following code below where we test if the shoot button was pressed in the PlayerEntity update() method:

```
if( ig.input.pressed('switch') ) {
    this.weapon ++;
    if(this.weapon >= this.totalWeapons)
        this.weapon = 0;
    switch(this.weapon){
```

```
            case(0):
                this.activeWeapon = "EntityBullet";
                break;
            case(1):
                this.activeWeapon = "EntityGrenade";
            break;
        }
    }
```

Now, when we go to spawn our weapon instance, we can simply check to see which weapon is set in the weapon property and spawn the correct instance.

We will also need to add a new property called this.activeWeapon to the top of our class:

```
activeWeapon: "EntityBullet",
```

Notice how we have to set the value to a string instead of a reference to the class itself? This will be evaluated correctly when the player class gets created. If we don't make the default value a string, it will break the player class when it tries to load.

The last thing we need to do is update our shoot code in the player class with the following:

```
if( ig.input.pressed('shoot') ) {
    ig.game.spawnEntity( this.activeWeapon, this.pos.x, this.pos.y, {flip:this.flip} );
}
```

This simply spawns a new instance of any class you have set as the this.active Weapon value. Now you are ready to test out your new grenade and switch between the two weapons.

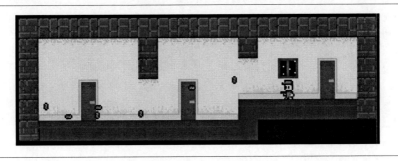

Figure 4-22. The player can now throw grenades.

You may have noticed that the player still looks like he has a gun in his hand and that there really aren't any visual changes when you switch weapons. We can quickly fix this by modifying how we set up our player's animations in the init() method. Go ahead and delete the four lines of code where we set up the idle, run, jump, and fall animations. Then add the following in its place:

```
this.setupAnimation(this.weapon);
```

Now we will create a new method called setupAnimation(), which takes our current weapon ID as an offset. Here is the code to add below the init() method:

```
setupAnimation: function(offset){
    offset = offset * 10;
    this.addAnim('idle', 1, [0+offset]);
    this.addAnim('run', .07, [0+offset,1+offset,2+offset,3+offset,4+offset,5+offset]);
    this.addAnim('jump', 1, [9+offset]);
    this.addAnim('fall', 0.4, [6+offset,7+offset]);
},
```

This is just like our original animation setup, except we now take the weapon ID (which becomes an offset), multiply it by the total number of player frames with a weapon, and add it to each animation. Let's look at the player sprite sheet so you can see what's going on.

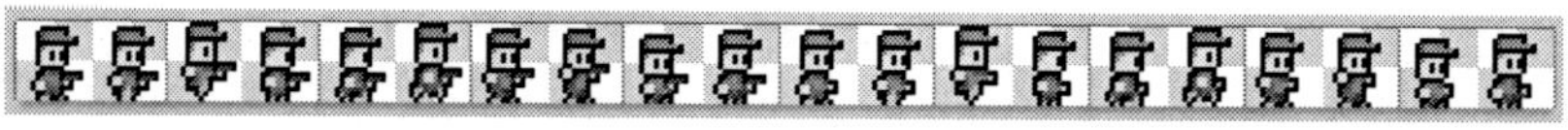

Figure 4-23. The player sprites with a gun and without one.

As you can see, we have 10 sprites holding a gun and 10 sprites without the gun. By offsetting the animation by 10 frames, we can easily switch between the different sets of sprites. This is a common trick, and one we will use later on when we add death animations. For now, we just need to add one last line of code to help update the player graphics when we switch weapons. Add a call to this.setupAnimation() at the end of where we test for the weapon switch key press:

```
switch(this.weapon){
    case(0):
            this.activeWeapon = "EntityBullet";
            break;
    case(1):
            this.activeWeapon = "EntityGrenade";
    break;
}
this.setupAnimation(this.weapon);
```

Now when you test and hit the Tab key, you should see the player's animation change based on the weapon he is using (Figure 4-24).

From here, you should be able to add even more weapons to your game by simply using the above pattern and building upon it.

Killing Entities

You may have noticed while we set up our weapons that we called a built-in method called kill(). While reducing an entity's life will destroy it and automatically call kill() for you, there are times when you may need to do this manually—like when the

Figure 4-24. Now you can see the player's sprite update when switching between weapons.

grenade collides with an enemy or it bounces too much. This method actually completely removes the entity from the render list, so it is a helpful way to permanently remove entities from the game. If you do not call kill() on anything you need to remove from the game, things will start to slow down considerably, so make sure you take advantage of the kill() method.

Respawning the Player

Since the player dies as soon as he collides with an enemy, we should add some logic to respawn the player. The easiest way to do this is to save out the start position of the player when he gets created so we can restore him to the same position when he dies. Let's add the following property to our PlayerEntity class:

```
startPosition: null,
```

Then, we can store the initial position of the player by adding the following to the init() method above the call to this.parent():

```
this.startPosition = {x:x,y:y};
```

What this does is save a generic object with the x,y position that gets passed into the constructor of our player class. Now, we just need to override the kill() method to this:

```
kill: function(){
    this.parent();
    ig.game.spawnEntity( EntityPlayer, this.startPosition.x, this.startPosition.y );
}
```

So, what will happen is that when kill() gets called after the player collides with a monster, we call this.parent(), which will properly remove the player instance from the game. Then, we immediately spawn a new player at the saved startPosition. Right now, it is a little jarring, but you could easily add a delay and then respawn after displaying some message to the user.

Another really cool trick about this approach is that since we saved the initial x,y position of the player in the startPosition property, we could easily update this value if the player walks through a checkpoint. This means that we don't need any complex logic to continually respawn the player throughout the level. All the logic is contained inside the player instance itself.

One thing you should pay special attention to is when a monster is on top of the respawn position. Since we don't reset the level, there is a chance that we could lock up the game if the monster kills the player as soon as he respawns, as shown in Figure 4-25.

Figure 4-25. Right now, a monster on our respawn position will lock up the game.

The same thing can happen if there are a lot of grenades bouncing around where the player respawns. Usually, games offer some sort of invincibility mode when the player restarts. Here is a quick example of how to do that. Start by adding the following two properties to our EntityPlayer class:

```
invincible: true,
invincibleDelay: 2,
invincibleTimer:null,
```

This will allow us to tell if the player is invincible, and also for how long. Next, we will need to add the following method to handle toggling the invincibility:

```
makeInvincible: function(){
    this.invincible = true;
    this.invincibleTimer.reset();
},
```

This will allow us to call makeInvincible() on the player at any time, and we can reset the invincibleTimer as well as toggle the invincible flag. Now we are going to have to override our receiveDamage() and draw() methods:

```
receiveDamage: function(amount, from){
    if(this.invincible)
        return;
    this.parent(amount, from);
},
draw: function(){
    if(this.invincible)
        this.currentAnim.alpha = this.invincibleTimer.delta()/this.invincibleDelay * 1 ;
    this.parent();
}
```

In the `receiveDamage()` method, we are using a guard clause to test if invincibility has been toggled and, if so, we just exit the method and don't apply any damage. In the draw method, we also test for invincibility and, if it is activated, we are going to set the `alpha` value of the sprite to reflect how much longer they are invincible. We start at 0 and they will slowly fade into the game. Alpha in Impact is a value between 0 and 1. We can easily find a percentage of that value by dividing the `invincibleTimer`'s delta by the `invincibleDelay`. By multiplying it by 1, the total value of alpha, we get a percentage that we can use to make the player fade in.

Before we can test this, we need to do two more things. First, we need to add the following to our `init()` method:

```
this.invincibleTimer = new ig.Timer();
this.makeInvincible();
```

Next, we need to add the following code to our `update()` method just before our call to `this.parent()`:

```
if( this.invincibleTimer.delta() > this.invincibleDelay ) {
    this.invincible = false;
    this.currentAnim.alpha = 1;
}
```

This basically tests to see if our timer is greater than the delay we defined. Once that happens, we disable invincibility by setting invincible to `false` and forcing the `alpha` to be 1. If you refresh, you should now see the player fade in when he is created and after you respawn.

Figure 4-26. When a new player is spawned, he is temporarily invincible.

This should fix the issue we had before (when the player respawns on top of a monster or grenade) so that we don't lock up the game. Also, because of the way this was set up, you can now call `makeInvincible()` at any time if you wanted to give the player a power-up or show that the player has taken damage without actually respawning him.

Create Death Animations

One of the easiest ways to show a death animation is to create a small particle explosion where the player is killed. Not only does this cut down on the amount of animations you have to create but you can also use the same technique to show damage taken by a projectile weapon. In order to do this, we will need to create two new entities, one for the explosion and the other for the actual particles. Let's add the following inner class to our `player.js` module:

```
EntityDeathExplosion = ig.Entity.extend({
    lifetime: 1,
    callBack: null,
    particles: 25,
    init: function( x, y, settings ) {
            this.parent( x, y, settings );
            for(var i = 0; i < this.particles; i++)
                    ig.game.spawnEntity(EntityDeathExplosionParticle, x, y, {colorOffset:
    settings.colorOffset ? settings.colorOffset : 0});
                    this.idleTimer = new ig.Timer();
    },
    update: function() {
            if( this.idleTimer.delta() > this.lifetime ) {
                this.kill();
                if(this.callBack)
                        this.callBack();
                return;
            }
    }
});
```

This is a very simple class. It handles spawning particle entities, which we will create next, and also has a timer, which we use to call a `callback()` method that is supplied by the setting property. Pay special attention to `this.idleTimer` and the new `ig.Timer()`. We use these to keep track of how much time has elapsed since its instantiation, just like we did when we added invincibility to the player.

There is also something else going on here. You may have noticed that when we spawn our `EntityDeathExplosionParticle`, we are passing in a color offset value. If you take a look at the blood sprite, you will see that we have colored sprites for the player in red and for the zombie in green.

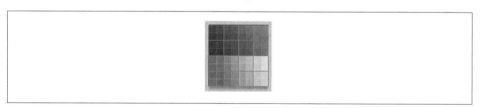

Figure 4-27. This sprite contains the player and zombie blood particles.

This is a neat trick and one that is used in a lot of sprite sheet-based games. Our blood particles are going to be 2×2 pixels in size. That means we have eight sprites for each color. When we set up our particle, we will apply the color offset to the graphic we display. So if the player is hit, we will add 0 to the `offset`, which will generate a random red color. For zombies we will add 1 to the `offset`, which will multiply by the base number of possible sprites and move the randomly selected sprite into the green zone.

Let's take a look at our particle class to see this in action. Create a new inner class with the following code:

```
EntityDeathExplosionParticle = ig.Entity.extend({
    size: {x: 2, y: 2},
    maxVel: {x: 160, y: 200},
    lifetime: 2,
    fadetime: 1,
    bounciness: 0,
    vel: {x: 100, y: 30},
    friction: {x:100, y: 0},
    collides: ig.Entity.COLLIDES.LITE,
    colorOffset: 0,
    totalColors: 7,
    animSheet: new ig.AnimationSheet( 'media/blood.png', 2, 2 ),
    init: function( x, y, settings ) {
        this.parent( x, y, settings );
        var frameID = Math.round(Math.random()*this.totalColors) + (this.colorOffset
 * (this.totalColors+1));
        this.addAnim( 'idle', 0.2, [frameID] );
        this.vel.x = (Math.random() * 2 - 1) * this.vel.x;
        this.vel.y = (Math.random() * 2 - 1) * this.vel.y;
        this.idleTimer = new ig.Timer();
    },
    update: function() {
        if( this.idleTimer.delta() > this.lifetime ) {
            this.kill();
            return;
        }
        this.currentAnim.alpha = this.idleTimer.delta().map(
            this.lifetime - this.fadetime, this.lifetime,
            1, 0
        );
        this.parent();
    }
});
```

As you can see, the particle has a few properties such as its maximum velocity, how long before it fades away, bounciness, and initial velocity. Most of this should look very familiar from what we did with our grenade class. As you can see in the init() method, we assign a random value to the particle's vel.x and vel.y values, which sends each one off in different directions. Since this is blood and we don't want it bouncing around like the grenade, the bounciness property is set to 0. We take advantage of this. currentAnim.alpha value, which assigns a new alpha value after each update, and eventually the particle disappears. Once it fades away, we call kill() to remove it from the display.

Now that we have our particle emitter and our particle, we can extend the player's kill() method to spawn our EntityDeathExplosion where the player was killed and watch it spawn random particles as if the player exploded. Here is the modified EntityPlayer kill() method:

```
kill: function(){
    this.parent();
    var x = this.startPosition.x;
    var y = this.startPosition.y;
    ig.game.spawnEntity(EntityDeathExplosion, this.pos.x, this.pos.y,
{callBack:function(){ig.game.spawnEntity( EntityPlayer, x, y)}} );
}
```

Since we are passing a function into the settings object, we will need to re-scope the start position of the player. If you refresh your browser and run the player into the monster, you will now see him explode into tiny pieces that bounce and fade away.

Figure 4-28. The player now explodes into pieces.

As I mentioned before, this is also a great effect for us to show when an entity has been hit. Let's override the `zombie.js` `receiveDamage()` method with the following:

```
receiveDamage: function(value){
    this.parent(value);
    if(this.health > 0)
        ig.game.spawnEntity(EntityDeathExplosion, this.pos.x, this.pos.y, {particles:
2, colorOffset: 1});
},
```

We can actually use the same death explosion class in our zombie entity, even though it is an inner class of player. This is a neat little hack thanks to the fact that JS's scope is global and, when any entity gets defined in Impact, it is available throughout the game engine. So, in the `EntityZombie` class, we simply spawn a new death explosion just like we did in the player class, but pass in a smaller number of particles to be emitted. We also pass in the `colorOffset` so that we can display green blood instead of red. Now when a bullet hits the zombie, little particles will shoot off of it. Also, don't forget to use the same death animation technique we used on the player by overriding the `zombie.js` `kill()` method with the following:

```
kill: function(){
    this.parent();
    ig.game.spawnEntity(EntityDeathExplosion, this.pos.x, this.pos.y, {colorOffset:
1});
}
```

And there you go; you have just created a nice-looking dynamic death animation for your player and monster. We can also apply the same technique to our grenades and make their explosions more visually appealing, so let's take a look.

Adding Grenade Explosions

Now that we have seen how to add death animations to our player and zombie, let's look at how to make our grenades explode. Let's add the following particle to our player.js module:

```
EntityGrenadeParticle = ig.Entity.extend({
    size: {x: 1, y: 1},
    maxVel: {x: 160, y: 200},
    lifetime: 1,
    fadetime: 1,
    bounciness: 0.3,
    vel: {x: 40, y: 50},
    friction: {x:20, y: 20},
    checkAgainst: ig.Entity.TYPE.B,
    collides: ig.Entity.COLLIDES.LITE,
    animSheet: new ig.AnimationSheet( 'media/explosion.png', 1, 1 ),
    init: function( x, y, settings ) {
        this.parent( x, y, settings );
        this.vel.x = (Math.random() * 4 - 1) * this.vel.x;
        this.vel.y = (Math.random() * 10 - 1) * this.vel.y;
        this.idleTimer = new ig.Timer();
        var frameID = Math.round(Math.random()*7);
        this.addAnim( 'idle', 0.2, [frameID] );
    },
    update: function() {
        if( this.idleTimer.delta() > this.lifetime ) {
            this.kill();
            return;
        }
        this.currentAnim.alpha = this.idleTimer.delta().map(
            this.lifetime - this.fadetime, this.lifetime,
            1, 0
        );
        this.parent();
    }
});
```

At this point, everything should look very familiar. We probably could have even extended our EntityDeathExplosionParticle but, to keep things simple, I just copied over the code and changed a few properties. Now we just need to spawn a few particles once the grenade explodes. Override the EntityGrenade kill() method with this code:

```
kill: function(){
    for(var i = 0; i < 20; i++)
        ig.game.spawnEntity(EntityGrenadeParticle, this.pos.x, this.pos.y);
    this.parent();
}
```

Refresh the game and fire a grenade. You should see a nice little particle explosion when it collides with anything or bounces too many times.

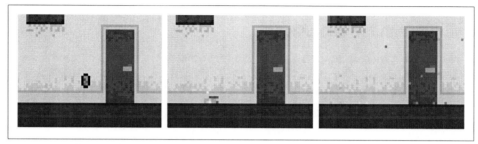

Figure 4-29. The grenade now explodes.

Customizing the Camera

Right now, our level is really boring. Impact was designed for side-scrolling games, so let's go back into our map editor and extend out the level so the player has some room to run around. Create an opening in the far right wall and add another room to the map. Make sure that you increase the size of the main layer and the collision layer as well.

Figure 4-30. The level after expanding it.

Once you have extended the level, save and try to play it. You may notice something isn't quite right (Figure 4-31).

Did you see that the game's camera is not following the player? We will need to set this up manually in the main.js class. Open it up and we will override the update function with the following code:

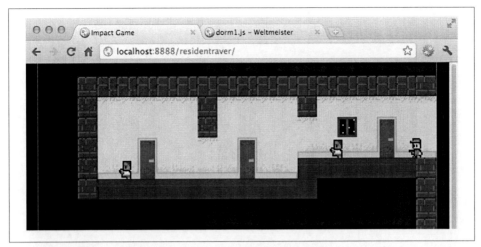

Figure 4-31. As you move through the level, the camera doesn't follow the player.

```
update: function() {
    // screen follows the player
    var player = this.getEntitiesByType( EntityPlayer )[0];
    if( player ) {
        this.screen.x = player.pos.x - ig.system.width/2;
        this.screen.y = player.pos.y - ig.system.height/2;
    }
    // Update all entities and BackgroundMaps
    this.parent();
},
```

The way that this code works is that we take advantage of a method of the game class called getEntitiesByType(). This is a very important API when it comes to finding instances of entities in your game. Because we know that there is only a single instance of our player, we can explicitly look for it. There are better ways of getting a reference to the player, but for now we will just use this technique to keep things simple.

After we see if the player exists, we can get the screen resolution and player position to center the screen's x,y values. By setting the screen.x and screen.y values, the renderer will automatically adjust the camera to that position. You can also do a lot of cool tricks with this, like easing the camera movement or limiting it so it doesn't scroll offscreen.

Now, refresh the game and you should see that the camera now follows our player as it moves through the level.

So, now that we have added the ability to move our camera around the level, it's time to allow the player to exit this level.

Figure 4-32. The camera following the player through the level.

Loading New Levels

It looks like we are ready to load our next level. Loading levels in Impact is incredibly easy; we actually did it as one of the first steps in setting up this game. In this section, I will talk about building something we call a trigger, which is an invisible area of the map that executes an activity when the player enters it. In this case, we will be building a level exit.

Let's start by creating a new entity file called `levelexit.js` and add the following code to it:

```
12    ig.module(
13        'game.entities.levelexit'
14    )
15    .requires(
16        'impact.entity'
17    )
18    .defines(function(){
19        EntityLevelexit = ig.Entity.extend({
20
21        });
22    });
```

Since our exit doesn't have any graphics, we still need something to display in Welt-meister. Let's add the following properties to our class:

```
_wmDrawBox: true,
_wmBoxColor: 'rgba(0, 0, 255, 0.7)',
size: {x: 8, y: 8},
```

These two properties with the `_wm` prefix tell Weltmeister how to render the object in the edit view, even though it doesn't have an actual graphic in the game. So, Weltmeister will draw an 8×8 pixel blue box.

Now, we need a way to store the name of the next level we should load when the player collides with the level exit entity. Add the following property, which will be automatically set during our entity's construction by the settings parameter we will pass in from the level data:

```
level: null,
```

Next, we just need to add some collision code. Let's have our level exit check against any `TYPE.A` entities by adding the following property to the top of your class:

```
checkAgainst: ig.Entity.TYPE.A,
```

Now, we will override `update()` and remove its call to `this.parent()` so we are not spending render cycles trying to draw an entity with no graphics. This is a great technique for any kind of triggers you may build for your map that aren't required to be updated visually on every frame:

```
update: function(){},
```

Finally, we will also override the `check()` method to handle the collision:

```
check: function( other ) {
    if(other instanceof EntityPlayer){
        if( this.level ) {
            var levelName = this.level.replace(/^(Level)?(\w)(\w*)/, function( m,
l, a, b ) {
            return a.toUpperCase() + b;
        });
            ig.game.loadLevelDeferred( ig.global['Level'+levelName] );
        }
    }
}
```

As you can see, we simply test that the instance of `other` (which is passed into the method during a collision) is an instance of the player's class. This helps avoid any other entity of `TYPE.A` you may have accidentally triggered in the level exit.

The last part of the code simply does a regex cleanup of the exit's `level` property to make sure it is capitalized correctly before calling `ig.game.loadLevelDeferred()`. This method is very important. You may remember that in our main class, it simply called `loadLevel()`. Well, `loadLevelDeferred()` waits until the main game's update loop is completed before loading the level. This will help avoid any sudden redraw errors that may happen when trying to exit in the middle of the render loop.

Once we have our new `EntityLevelexit`, we can open up Weltmeister and create a small exit to place our entity in.

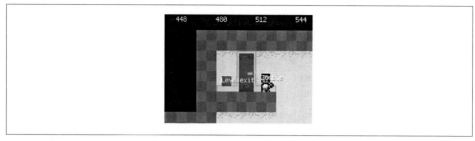

Figure 4-33. Now we can see where we placed the level exit in the editor.

When you add the level exit, you will need to tell it what level to load. Click on it and go to the layer area just under where it says Entity Settings. You should see all the properties of your entity instance. For the Key, put level and in Value, put dorm2.

Figure 4-34. Setting up a level property on the LevelExit entity.

It is very important that you hit Enter/Return after adding a value to an entity's Key, or it will not be saved. You will know it has been saved when you see the new Key/Value listed under the entity's name and its x,y values, which are set up by default. You can modify any Key by clicking on it.

Figure 4-35. Modifying entity properties in the level editor.

Now that our entity is configured, we need to create a new level. Name your level dorm2 and design it as shown in Figure 4-36.

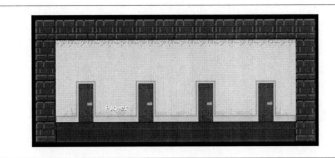

Figure 4-36. The second level of our game.

As you build out your new level you may notice that the player graphic is missing in the editor. This happens because now our player is set to invincible when he is created, so he is invisible. If this is an issue, you can add the following two properties to your `player.js` class:

```
_wmDrawBox: true,
_wmBoxColor: 'rgba(255, 0, 0, 0.7)',
```

This will render out a red box for the player when in the editor, just like we did with our level edit.

Figure 4-37. We use a red box to display the invisible player in the level editor.

The last thing you need to do is add the level and the level exit to the `main.js` `requires` block:

```
'game.levels.dorm2,
```

Once you have done this, refresh your game and you should be able to exit the level and go into the second level.

You may notice that the transition is a little jarring. There are a few things you can do to make sure that doesn't happen, such as matching the level exit and spawn points up, or building a quick transition before exiting the level. Usually, games have an end-of-level summary screen that gets displayed, so that when the next level loads up the player doesn't notice the transition as much. We'll talk more about this later in the book.

CHAPTER 5

Working With Text

It is relatively easy to work with text in Impact. If you remember back to our default main class, we had removed an instance of font class from the game—but in this section, we are going to talk about adding it back in and how to customize text at runtime.

Creating Font Sprite Sheets

Since Impact renders all the graphics to the page's Canvas tag, we will not be able to use system fonts. Instead, Impact uses a special sprite sheet for each font. Figure 5-1 is an example of the default font 04b03.font.png, which comes with the template project.

Figure 5-1. Impact's default font sprite sheet.

As you can see, all the font's characters are laid out horizontally with one pixel line under each character, which defines the width of that character. Figure 5-2 is a close-up of a few characters from the sprite sheet.

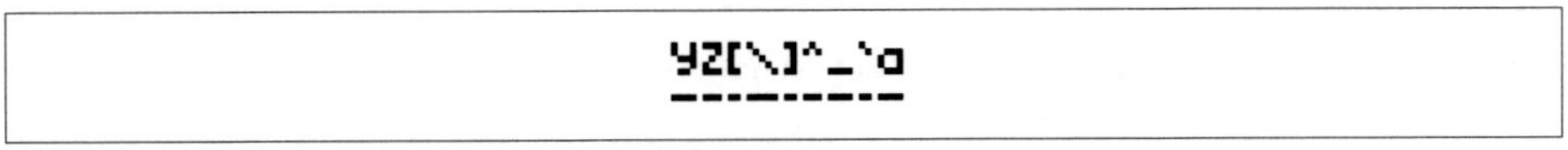

Figure 5-2. Notice the black lines under each character.

All fonts you want to use in Impact must be set up in a similar way. Luckily, there is an online tool to help generate new font sprite sheets, which you can test at *http:// impactjs.com/font-tool/*.

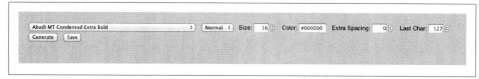

Figure 5-3. Impact's online font sprite sheet generation tool.

This tool allows you to select one of your system fonts and tweak its style, size, and thickness then generate a new font sprite sheet. Just click Generate when you are ready and download the new font sprite sheet. Once you have your new font, simply put it in your game's media folder, and you should be ready to use it. Make sure you add the `.font.png` extension to the generated image so that Impact knows it is dealing with a bitmap font.

Adding Text to Your Game

Now that we have seen how to create new fonts for our game, let's take a look at putting some text in our game. We are going to show a simple message at the bottom of the screen that tells the player what the controls are when they enter our level. Once the player moves, we will remove the instructions. Open up `main.js` and add the following property just below where we define our game's gravity:

```
instructText: new ig.Font( 'media/04b03.font.png' ),
```

We will also need to import the font class, so add the following to our `requires` code block:

```
'impact.font'
```

Finally, we are going to have to render this text on each frame, so add the following under the call to `this.parent()` in the `draw()` method:

```
draw: function() {
    // Draw all entities and backgroundMaps
    this.parent();
    var x = ig.system.width/2,
    y = ig.system.height - 10;
    this.instructText.draw(
    'Left/Right Moves, X Jumps, C Fires & Tab Switches Weapons.',
    x, y, ig.Font.ALIGN.CENTER );
}
```

As you can see, we first calculate the `x,y` position to render the text. We can use `ig.system` to find out the game's width and height, so we can center the text and display it on the bottom of the screen. There are three supported font alignments:

```
ig.Font.ALIGN.LEFT
ig.Font.ALIGN.RIGHT
ig.Font.ALIGN.CENTER
```

Next, we tell the font to render by calling draw and passing in the text it should display and its position, as well as how to align the text. It should look like Figure 5-4.

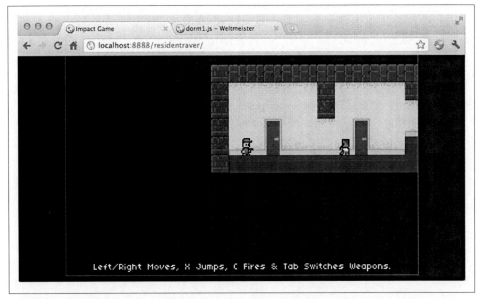

Figure 5-4. The player will see the game's controls when it's loaded up for the first time.

Now we want to make this text disappear once the player starts moving. To do this, we need to wrap the code we just placed in a conditional like this:

```
if(this.instructText){
    var x = ig.system.width/2,
    y = ig.system.height - 10;
    this.instructText.draw(
    'Left/Right Moves, X Jumps, C Fires & Tab Switches Weapons.',
    x, y, ig.Font.ALIGN.CENTER );
}
```

This will test to make sure an instance of the instructionText font exists before trying to render it. Now we can add some simple logic to remove the instructions as soon as the player moves. Add the following code just below where we test if the player instance exits if(player) in the main.js update() method:

```
if( player ) {
    this.screen.x = player.pos.x - ig.system.width/2;
    this.screen.y = player.pos.y - ig.system.height/2;
    if(player.accel.x > 0 && this.instructText)
        this.instructText = null;
}
```

This code tests to see if the player's acceleration increases, which happens when the player moves. Once the player is moving and if the font instance exists, we set it to null. After the other update we made in the draw method, which tests if the font instance exists, we basically tell the draw loop to ignore rendering the font, and it disappears.

While this is an incredibly crude example of how to show instructions when we start a level, it is a good basis for how you can add additional text or even messages during your game. Keep in mind that working with bitmap fonts is very limiting. If you want to have different colors, you will need to generate new font sprite sheets with those colors. Another great way to display text in your game is to use JavaScript to write to a div that sits above your game. While you will be limited to web fonts unless you embed a font in your HTML wrapper page, this approach allows you to create more complex-looking messages with HTML and JavaScript.

CHAPTER 6

Working With Sound

Impact also supports sound as well as background music for your game. In this chapter, we will learn how to add sound effects, background music, and learn a little more about browser compatibility issues.

Adding Sounds

In order to add sound to our game, we are going to have to use the `ig.Sound` class. Impact supports two file formats: `Ogg Vorbis` and `MP3`. The `ig.SoundManager` class can automatically detect which file to load based on the browser. Here are some examples of how to set up an `ig.Sound` instance:

```
var sound = new ig.Sound( 'media/sounds/jump.ogg' );
var sound = new ig.Sound( 'media/sounds/jump.mp3' );
var sound = new ig.Sound( 'media/sounds/jump.*' );
```

The last example is a wild card that lets the `ig.SoundManager` automatically load the correct file for us. Our sound files, just like images, should live inside the media directory. I also keep them in a subdirectory called *sounds*, so they stay organized. Let's add some sound effects to our player. Open the `player.js` class and set up the following properties at the top of our player class:

```
jumpSFX: new ig.Sound( 'media/sounds/jump.*' ),
shootSFX: new ig.Sound( 'media/sounds/shoot.*' ),
deathSFX: new ig.Sound( 'media/sounds/death.*' ),
```

Now we need to play the sound for each of these actions. Add the following line to the code where our player jumps:

```
if( this.standing && ig.input.pressed('jump')){
    this.vel.y = -this.jump;
    this.jumpSFX.play();
}
```

Next, we want to add a sound effect to our shoot animation. Locate the code where we fire our weapon and add the following line:

```
if( ig.input.pressed('shoot') ) {
    ig.game.spawnEntity( this.activeWeapon, this.pos.x, this.pos.y, {flip:this.flip} );
    this.shootSFX.play();
}
```

When you build out your full game, you may want to have different sound effects for each weapon, but for this section we are going to keep things simple. Now we need our death sound. Locate where we overrode `kill()` and add the following line of code:

```
kill: function(){
        this.deathSFX.play();
        this.parent();
```

The last thing we need to do, if you haven't done it already, is import the `ig.Sound` class in the `requires` block of the `player.js` class.

```
.requires(
    'impact.entity',
    'impact.sound'
)
```

We should be ready to test out our sound effects now. Open up the browser and refresh the game. There should now be sound, and Impact handles all the messy sound logic for you. It couldn't be any easier than this! Now let's look at adding some background music to our game.

Adding Music

Our game is a little boring without some background music. Luckily, Impact supports looping background music right out of the box. All we need to do is tell the music class what files to load and set the volume then call `play()`. Let's go back into our `main.js` class and add the following at the beginning of the `init()` method:

```
ig.music.add( 'media/sounds/theme.*' );
ig.music.volume = 0.5;
ig.music.play();
```

Unlike playing sound effects, we will talk directly to the music class. We can add tracks to the music class, which will help us switch between different background music as we move through our game. Since we are only setting up one track, it will automatically get selected when you call `play()`. You can add more tracks via the `add()` method and select a track by calling `ig.music.track()` and passing in the ID of the track you want to play.

That is all there is to playing background music in your game. Before we move on, we should talk a little bit about browser compatibility and set expectations for when sounds will work and when it's best not to play them.

Mobile Browser Sound Compatibility Issues

HTML5 audio is still in the early stages of being implemented across each browser. As you have seen, we still need to supply two different audio formats, and there is a good chance that a browser may not even support audio at all. This happens more on mobile than desktop browsers, but it's still a good thing to keep in mind when setting up your audio.

To play it safe, you may just want to totally disable sound on mobile. You can do this with the following code in your main game module right before where we start our game:

```
if( ig.ua.mobile ) {
    // Disable sound for all mobile devices
    ig.Sound.enabled = false;
}

// Start the game
ig.main(...)
```

By setting ig.Sound.enabled to false, no sound files will be loaded or played back. If you don't disable sounds on mobile browsers that don't support audio correctly, your game may try to load and crash, or hang in the pre-loader screen. Also, setting sound to false is incredibly helpful when you are testing your game over and over again.

CHAPTER 7

Creating Game Screens and HUDs

Every game needs screens. These are usually displayed at the beginning and end of the game, along with additional screens like credits and settings. In this section, we are going to go over creating three simple screens for our game, and I'll show you how to connect them all.

Extending Impact's Game Class

When it comes to creating game screens, there are several approaches you can take. Use HTML to display elements on top of your game and never build any of the game screens inside of Impact; or you could easily use divs and control them via jQuery and even directly with JavaScript; or you can make your screen from custom-built levels with entities as graphics in them and use some kind of level-loading manager to switch between them. The advantages would be having one game class and being able to use the level editor to create your screens. The downside would be that any custom code you have to run your level in the game class would also run while in a game screen.

The approach I find works the best is to simply create new ig.Game classes and switch between them. This allows you to create encapsulated custom logic to handle each different game screen while maintaining code separation, as well as being able to build upon your own base game screen class. We briefly touched on Impact's Game class early on in the book, but didn't talk about how it really works under the hood or how you can use it to create different screens in your game.

The ig.Game class represents the active view of your game. Right now our game class shows our level, player, and monsters, but could just as easily display a start screen or anything else. When our main.js class extends it, we supply some logic to run our game, but as you will see in the next section, we can also extend the ig.Game class to handle all of our in-game screens.

Perhaps the most important thing to keep in mind when working with the Game class is that you can display a new one by calling ig.system.setGame() and passing it a reference to the Game class you want to use. This allows us to quickly switch between game screens at any time. As our first example, let's take a look at how to set up a simple start screen.

Creating a Start Screen

In order to create our start screen, we are going to need to extend the ig.Game class. We can actually set up each of our game's screens as inner classes in our main.js file just like we did with other entities in our game. This also allows you to keep all your game screens organized in one file. Add the following code to our main.js module right after the end of our MyGame class but before the ig.main constructor:

```
46              this.instructText.draw( 'Left/Righ
47        }
48      }
49   });
50
51   if( ig.ua.mobile ) {
52        // Disable sound for all mobile devices
53        ig.Sound.enabled = false;
54   }
55
56   // Start the Game with 60fps, a resolution of
57   // up by a factor of 2
58   ig.main( '#canvas', MyGame, 60, 320, 240, 2 );
59
60   });
```

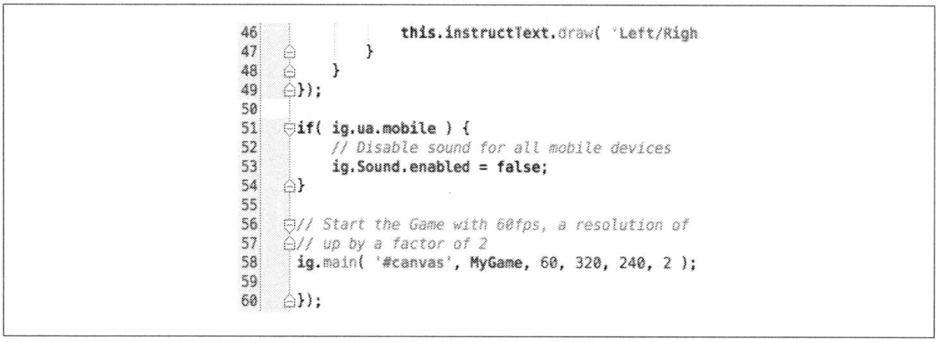

Figure 7-1. You want to start your start screen inner class right before the ig.main constructor.

Here is the StartScreen class code:

```
StartScreen = ig.Game.extend({
    instructText: new ig.Font( 'media/04b03.font.png' ),
    background: new ig.Image('media/screen-bg.png'),
    init: function() {
        ig.input.bind( ig.KEY.SPACE, 'start');
    },
    update: function() {
        if(ig.input.pressed ('start')){
            ig.system.setGame(MyGame)
        }
        this.parent();
    },
    draw: function() {
        this.parent();
        this.background.draw(0,0);
        var x = ig.system.width/2,
        y = ig.system.height - 10;
        this.instructText.draw( 'Press Spacebar To Start', x+40, y,
ig.Font.ALIGN.CENTER );
    }
});
```

This should look very familiar to you at this point. We simply extend the ig.Game class, then override a few methods. In init(), we bind the space bar key to start so we can listen for the moment the user is ready to play the game. Next, we override the update method to handle the space bar being pressed. As soon as we detect that the space bar has been pressed, we tell the ig.system class to load the MyGame class. Finally, in our draw() method, we draw a background image to the display, then add some text on top of it.

Before we can preview our start screen, we need to change the game init() code at the bottom of our main.js class to the following:

```
ig.main( '#canvas', StartScreen, 60, 320, 240, 2 );
```

As you can see, we now load the StartScreen class by default. If you refresh your game, you should see something like Figure 7-2.

Figure 7-2. Our game's start screen.

If you hit the space bar, you should be taken into your game. Now whenever we want to change the game screen we can simply call ig.system.setGame() and pass in the reference of the game class we want to display.

Before we move on, we should add a few more graphics to our StartScreen class since it looks really boring. Let's add the following two images as properties at the top of the StartScreen class:

```
mainCharacter: new ig.Image('media/screen-main-character.png'),
title: new ig.Image('media/game-title.png'),
```

Next, we will need to draw these two images to the display. Put the following code below where we call draw on our background image, and before our `instructionText` draw call:

```
this.background.draw(0,0);
this.mainCharacter.draw(0,0);
this.title.draw(ig.system.width - this.title.width, 0);
```

Now if you refresh, you should see something like Figure 7-3.

Figure 7-3. We now have some graphics on our start screen background.

This looks a lot better! Since each image is now rendered on its own, you could do some cool things like fade each one up or make them slide in. Simply play around with their x,y position or alpha on the `update()` method to modify where and how they get drawn to the display. Now let's look at how we can add in a stats screen to display at the end of a level.

Player Stats Screen

Next up, we are going to look at how we can keep track of player stats such as the time it took to complete a level, total number of kills, and how many times the player died.

Instead of making this screen a separate game class, we are going to build it into our MyGame class.

We are going to need to add impact.timer to the requires block of our MyGame class. Add the following properties to the MyGame class:

```
statText: new ig.Font( 'media/04b03.font.png' ),
showStats: false,
statMatte: new ig.Image('media/stat-matte.png'),
levelTimer: new ig.Timer(),
levelExit: null,
stats: {time: 0, kills: 0, deaths: 0},
```

The following properties will allow us to track the visibility of the stats display, an image we can use to mask the screen, a font, a timer, and a stats object. Next, we are going to need to override the loadLevel() method so we can start a timer to track how long it takes the player to complete the level:

```
loadLevel: function( data ) {
    this.parent(data);
    this.levelTimer.reset();
},
```

This basically resets the timer when the main game class has loaded a level. Now in order to display our screen, we have to pause the update loop. The easiest way to do this will be to wrap the call to this.parent() inside update() with a conditional. Here is what the new this.parent() code should look like inside of update():

```
// Update all entities and BackgroundMaps
if(!this.showStats){
    this.parent();
}else{
    if(ig.input.state('continue')){
        this.showStats = false;
        this.levelExit.nextLevel();
        this.parent();
    }
}
```

Now we are testing to see if it's time to show the stats screen. If it is not being displayed, we call this.parent() and the game runs like normal. If the stats display is visible, we delay the call to this.parent() and listen for an input state of continue. Basically, we want the player to press the space bar to remove the stats screen and continue on. Let's set up the new key listener underneath where we bound all of our other gameplay keys in the init() method:

```
ig.input.bind( ig.KEY.SPACE, 'continue' );
```

Now we need to add in the logic to display our game stats. We can do this by adding the following to our draw() method:

```
if(this.showStats){
    this.statMatte.draw(0,0);
    var x = ig.system.width/2;
```

```
var y = ig.system.height/2 - 20;
this. statText.draw('Level Complete', x, y, ig.Font.ALIGN.CENTER);
this. statText.draw('Time: '+this.stats.time, x, y+30, ig.Font.ALIGN.CENTER);
this. statText.draw('Kills: '+this.stats.kills, x, y+40, ig.Font.ALIGN.CENTER);
this. statText.draw('Deaths: '+this.stats.deaths, x, y+50, ig.Font.ALIGN.CENTER);
this. statText.draw('Press Spacebar to continue.', x, ig.system.height - 10,
ig.Font.ALIGN.CENTER);
}
```

Again, we are testing if we should be showing the stats. Once the stats have been toggled to display, we render out all the elements that make up the screen, starting with the background image, by calling this.statMatte.draw(0,0). Our stat matte is just a black image set to 80% transparent. By using an image for the background overlay, you can make this look any way you want. From there, we calculate the base x,y positions where we want to start rendering our text. Next, we use statText to render text on top of the stat matte. Notice how we reuse the same font reference each time? This is a good trick to help you cut down on memory and limit the amount of fonts we need to keep track of, since they are all the same style.

Before we can test our screen, we will need to set up a method to toggle our stat screen. Add the following method to the MyGame class:

```
toggleStats: function(levelExit){
    this.showStats = true;
    this.stats.time = Math.round(this.levelTimer.delta());
    this.levelExit = levelExit;
}
```

Now we have everything we need to track our stats and display them when we complete the level. Let's modify our EntityLevelexit class's check function to this:

```
check: function(other) {
    if (other instanceof EntityPlayer) {
        ig.game.toggleStats(this);
    }
},
```

From here, you can see that we still test whether the player has collided with the level exit, so we directly call toggleStats on the ig.game class. Notice how we pass a reference of the level exit to the toggleStats method? This allows the game class to call the nextLevel() method on the EntityLevelexit instance, which we need to add right now:

```
nextLevel: function(){
    if (this.level) {
        var levelName = this.level.replace(/^(Level)?(\w)(\w*)/, function(m, l, a, b) {
        return a.toUpperCase() + b;
    });
        ig.game.loadLevelDeferred(ig.global['Level' + levelName]);
    }
}
```

Now you have everything you need to display level complete stats. Let's give our game a quick test and see what happens.

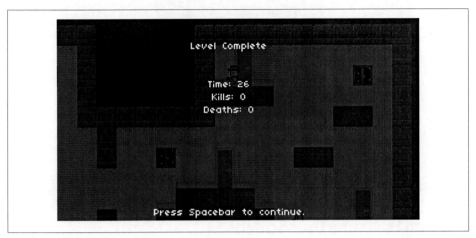

Figure 7-4. Our level complete screen with player stats.

As you can see, we now have the foundation for our stats screen, but we need to tell our player class what stats to track. Since we already set up a simple object to track stats in our game class, all we need to do is modify the `ig.game.stats` object to reflect the new values. Let's open up the `player.js` class and add some code to track the number of deaths. Add the following line to the `kill()` method:

```
ig.game.stats.deaths ++;
```

This will increase the `deaths` value by 1 each time the player dies. Next, we want to track each kill. Open our `zombie.js` class and add the following to its `kill()` method:

```
ig.game.stats.kills ++;
```

Now every time we kill a monster, we increase the `kills` value by 1. The last thing we need to do is be able to reset our game stats when a new level is loaded. Open up the `main.js` class and add the following to our `loadLevel()` method above the call to `this.parent()`:

```
this.stats = {time: 0, kills: 0, deaths: 0};
```

This will reset the stats object every time a new level is loaded. Reload the game and see if your stats are working. You should see your final level stats updated to reflect the time, kills, and deaths properly.

Figure 7-5. Now our stats display the correct number of zombie kills and player deaths.

Let's look at how to handle our game over screen.

Creating the Game Over Screen

So far we are tracking how many times the player dies, but not the number of lives the player has. We also don't have a way to handle what happens when he runs out of those lives. Before we create our Game Over screen, let's add a new property to the MyGame class in the main.js file:

```
lives: 3,
```

Now we are ready to show a Game Over screen. This is going to be similar to how we set up our start screen. Let's create a new inner class in our main.js file right below our StartScreen, called GameOverScreen:

```
GameOverScreen = ig.Game.extend({
    instructText: new ig.Font( 'media/04b03.font.png' ),
    background: new ig.Image('media/screen-bg.png'),
    gameOver: new ig.Image('media/game-over.png'),
    stats: {},
    init: function() {
        ig.input.bind( ig.KEY.SPACE, 'start');
        this.stats = ig.finalStats;
    },
    update: function() {
        if(ig.input.pressed('start')){
            ig.system.setGame(StartScreen)
        }
        this.parent();
    },
    draw: function() {
        this.parent();
        this.background.draw(0,0);
        var x = ig.system.width/2;
        var y = ig.system.height/2 - 20;
        this.gameOver.draw(x - (this.gameOver.width * .5), y - 30);
        var score = (this.stats.kills * 100) - (this.stats.deaths * 50);
```

```
        this.instructText.draw('Total Kills: '+this.stats.kills, x, y+30,
ig.Font.ALIGN.CENTER);
        this.instructText.draw('Total Deaths: '+this.stats.deaths, x, y+40,
ig.Font.ALIGN.CENTER);
        this.instructText.draw('Score: '+score, x, y+50, ig.Font.ALIGN.CENTER);
        this.instructText.draw('Press Spacebar To Continue.', x, ig.system.height -
10, ig.Font.ALIGN.CENTER);
    }
});
```

This is just like our StartGame class, except we are displaying a few different images and also want to show the player's final score and stats. Once the player hits the space bar, it will go back to the start screen. Next, we will need to modify the player.js class to call the GameOverScreen when the player runs out of lives. We are going to have to replace the player's kill() method in player.js with the following:

```
kill: function(){
    this.deathSFX.play();
    this.parent();
    ig.game.respawnPosition = this.startPosition;
    ig.game.spawnEntity(EntityDeathExplosion, this.pos.x, this.pos.y,
{callBack:this.onDeath} );
},
```

We will also need to add the following new method to our EntityPlayer class player.js module:

```
onDeath: function(){
    ig.game.stats.deaths ++;
    ig.game.lives --;
    if(ig.game.lives < 0){
        ig.game.gameOver();
    }else{
        ig.game.spawnEntity( EntityPlayer, ig.game.respawnPosition.x,
ig.game.respawnPosition.y);
    }
},
```

Now when the player's kill() method is called, we simply spawn a new death explosion and have it call onDeath() as its callback. The onDeath() method handles updating our stats, subtracting from our lives value in the main game class, and determines if the game is over or if we should respawn the player. You may also notice that we store the player's startPosition in the Game class, since our onDeath() method will lose scope of the player's instance when kill() was called. We could make this cleaner by allowing our callback logic to accept a parameter object with values for the start position, but I wanted to keep the code as simple as possible. The last thing we need to do is add the gameOver() method. We just need to add this to the MyGame class:

```
gameOver: function(){
    ig.finalStats = ig.game.stats;
    ig.system.setGame(GameOverScreen);
}
```

We are doing a neat little trick here, thanks to the fact that JavaScript is a dynamic language. As you can see, we are going to take our game instance's stats object and add it to the `ig` class instance, which represents the root of our game's scope. This allows us to retrieve the last stats object from the game without having to pass it into the `GameOverScreen` class. Unfortunately, Impact doesn't allow us to pass values into new game classes when we create them via the `ig.system.setGame()` method, so we have to cheat. Now if you hit refresh and kill the player a few times you should see the screen in Figure 7-6.

Figure 7-6. Our Game Over screen.

As you can see, everything works great and our `GameOverScreen` should be getting the correct values to display the game stats and calculate the final score.

Adding In-Game HUD

The last thing we want to add into our game is going to be some kind of simple display showing how many lives we have left. We are going to keep our game's HUD (heads up display) as simple as possible. Let's go into our `MyGame` class and add the following property:

```
lifeSprite: new ig.Image('media/life-sprite.png'),
```

Next, we'll have to display these icons in our `draw()` method. Add the following to the end of the MyGame `draw()` method:

```
this.statText.draw("Lives", 5,5);
for(var i=0; i < this.lives; i++)
    this.lifeSprite.draw(((this.lifeSprite.width + 2) * i)+5, 15);
```

It couldn't get any easier than this. All we do here is create a new sprite for our life graphic. Then we use the `statText` instance to render out a label above a row of lives we render out in the for loop. By looping through the total number of lives that the player has left over, we can quickly lay them out horizontally. This is a great trick; simply multiply the sprite's width plus any padding by i from the for loop. This will stack the sprites horizontally and, by adding an additional 5px of padding to the value, we offset everything so it lines up right under the label text.

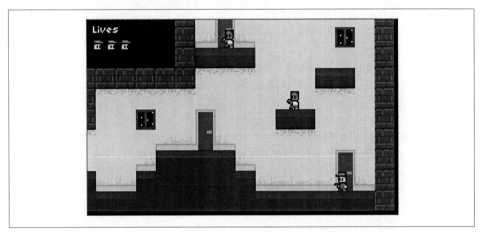

Figure 7-7. The new HUD shows the player how many lives he has left.

Now when the player loses a life, the draw loop automatically updates the display with the correct number of lives left. You can add all kinds of stats to this display—including the score, kills, or even a mini-map—by building off of this technique and HUD render block in our updated `draw()` method.

Game Rewards

Now that we have our screens in place, I want to outline a few reward systems that you should keep in mind as you build out your own game. Over the years, games have evolved from having simple high scores tables to complex unlocking reward systems. In the casual gaming space, rewarding players for continuing to play the game is a must. Let's take a look at some simple reward systems you can implement in your game:

Level selection

Allowing users to pick the levels they want to play and unlocking new ones the further they go in the game.

Steps to completion

While playing through a game, show the user how many steps are needed in order to complete the level or game. Showing progress helps players set their own goals and achieve them.

Scores

High scores are one of the most basic reward systems around and should be in every game. Allowing the player to compete against others or even their own best scores helps increase replay value.

Stats

Players love statistics about what they have done in the game. Showing totals of how many monsters have been killed or how may times they died can also help encourage the player to work on increasing the important stats that matter to them.

Badges

Giving the player reminders of their greatest achievements is an excellent way of rewarding them, and allows them to have something to keep and collect as they play the game.

Competition

Playing against other players is a great way to challenge players and offers up an ever-changing difficulty level that in-game AI would never be able to match.

Ranking

Along with scores and stats should be some kind of ranking. Let the player know how well they are doing and have that information shared among all the people playing your game.

In-game currency

Allowing players to buy in-game items that can help them clear a level or customize a character is not only a great reward for players, but may also be an excellent way to make some additional money.

Adding any number of these systems in your game will help ensure players have a good time as well as increase the re-playability of your game.

In-Game Analytics

The last thing I want to talk about when building out sections and stats for your game is keeping track of in-game analytics. In-game analytics are probably one of the most important things you can add as a developer, especially if you are testing out your game with a new audience. The following will serve as a good example of the kinds of things I am tracking and how I was able to adjust my development around people's feedback, as well as providing a good basis for real usage data that you can cross-reference.

The following figures come from a small game I launched in November 2010, and we are looking at the most important stats collected up until February 2011. This is an overview of my in-game usage. It's important to note that every Pageview is the user going to a new screen in the game. You should always be aware of the possible performance impact adding analytics may have on your game, so I try to add them when there is very little action going on in the game.

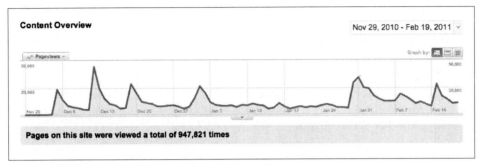

Figure 7-8. Google Analytics on my game from November 2010 to February 2011.

It's important to note the spikes here. These spikes in usage directly correlate to updates I have made to the game. Every update sees a huge uptake, then it quickly tapers off. I have found that releasing an update on Sunday afternoon/night is the best time of the week, and by Friday I would see a large drop in plays. Being able to release new content or updates for your game on a consistent basis is critical for keeping your game up on the charts and getting more users interested in sticking around long enough to continue playing. This is even more important if you are doing an ad-based distribution model, where needing to get lots of impressions is critical to making any kind of money.

Now, let's look at a more granular breakdown of these stats.

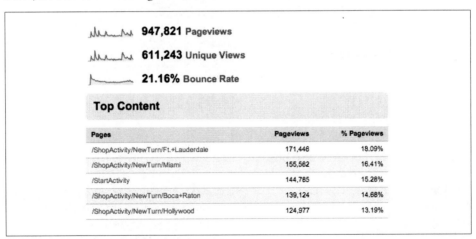

Figure 7-9. A deeper look at my game's stats.

As you can see, I was getting a large number of Pageviews with a really high number of Unique Views, which is really what you are looking for. Below these figures are the top pages or, in this case, activities being visited by users. Switching locations in the game ended the turn, but what is interesting to see is that Ft. Lauderdale is always going to come out on top; because that is where you start (plus your safe house/bank is there), the player will tend to travel closer to that location. The StartActivity is also high because the game is relatively short, so you end up playing more games. There are actually 5 locations in the game, so we can easily see which locations are popular and which are not. By using data like this, you can begin to determine parts of the game or locations that people avoid and add in new game systems to entice people to visit (or just drop those unpopular parts of the game).

The other thing that Google Analytics does very well is help track events. Games are full of all kinds of events, so I try to track as much as possible. As you can see, there are a large number of events going on during each game.

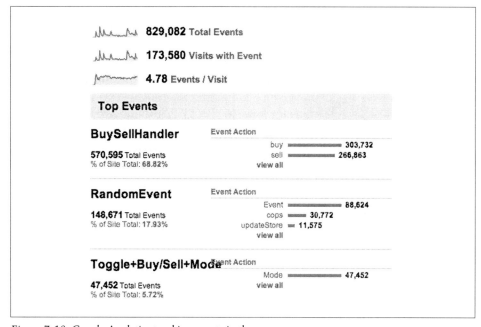

Figure 7-10. Google Analytics tracking events in the game.

Since the point of this game is to buy and sell items, we are going to see the majority of events revolve around the BuySellHandler, which is called every time a transaction is made. You can even see I track each one separately. Next up are random events that happen when you end a turn and go to a new location. These are super-common. I actually track which events show up, so I can tell if one event is just not working very well or needs a programmatic fix to make it appear more often. Finally, I also track UI events like when people click on buttons such as toggling between the buy and sell mode. This allows me to know if users are taking advantage of the UI or finding alternative ways to interact with the game mechanics.

Here are some more details about events in the game. As you can see, I am tracking the number of new games started, exits, and game overs so I can quickly pull up percentages to see if the game is too difficult (based on a comparison of starts versus completed games). If you don't see a lot of completed game events, this is a good indicator that your game isn't engaging enough or it's just too hard.

	Total Events **829,082** % of Site Total: 100.00%	Unique Events **251,155** % of Site Total: 100.00%	Event Value **342,921,886** % of Site Total: 100.00%	Avg. Value **413.62** Site Avg: 413.62 (0.00%)
Event Category	None	Total Events ↓	Unique Events	Event Value	Avg. Value

	Event Category	Total Events ↓	Unique Events	Event Value	Avg. Value
1.	BuySellHandler	570,595	109,673	47,515,916	83.27
2.	RandomEvent	148,671	75,789	323,218	2.17
3.	Toggle+Buy/Sell+Mode	47,452	7,224	70,867	1.49
4.	NewGame	26,772	27,360	13,485	0.47
5.	New+Version	10,379	10,076	10,379	1.00
6.	GameOver	9,419	7,820	294,979,591	31,317.51
7.	Exit	8,430	8,078	8,430	1.00
8.	ContinueGame	5,364	5,135	0	0.00

Filter Event Category: containing — Go — Advanced Filter — Go to: 1 — Show rows: 10 — 1 - 8 of 8

Figure 7-11. All in-game events. Notice the NewGame and GameOver events to track how many people complete the game.

This is a really quick overview of how analytics work in your game. When used correctly, it can help you find parts of your game that work and can help you locate areas that don't. Also, one of the added bonuses of making an HTML5 game is being able to work directly with Google Analytics' JS API right out of the box. Find more information on how to integrate Google Analytics into your JS game here: *http://code.google.com/apis/analytics*.

CHAPTER 8

Debugging Your Game

Impact's Debugger

As our game comes together and we begin to add more entities, performance is going to become a concern. Also, there may be things we need to see, such as the bounding boxes of entities and how many entities are on the screen at any given time. Luckily for us, there is a really great debugger built into Impact. In order to use it, we will need to add the following class to the `main.js` `requires` block:

```
'impact.debug.debug'
```

Once you have added this, refresh the game in your browser and you should now see the debug menu on the bottom of the screen.

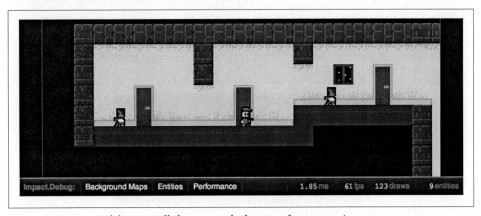

Figure 8-1. Impact's debugger will show up at the bottom of your game's page.

As you can see, the debugger has some very helpful features. On the right-hand side, you will see the number of milliseconds your code takes to execute on each frame, followed by the frames per second, draws, and finally the number of entities. On the left are options to explore the map layers, individual entities, and performance. Let's take a deeper look, starting with the map layers.

Figure 8-2. The Background Maps tab of the debugger shows us all of our map layers and a preview of the entire map.

Here, you can see a preview of your entire map and what is currently being rendered in the display. You can also turn off layers to help see what is going on or toggle some of the other map options such as Pre Rendered and Show Chunks. Now, let's look at the Entities tab.

Figure 8-3. The Entities tab contains all the debug options to help you manage your entities in the level.

Here, we can see some additional information about each entity. The two important ones are Show Collision Boxes and Show Velocities. Turn on Show Collision Boxes.

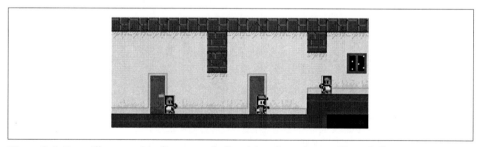

Figure 8-4. You will see a red outline around all entities after selecting Show Collision Boxes.

With Show Collision Boxes turned on, we can see each entity's bounding box, which is used to detect collisions. Remember how we changed the `.size` and `.offset` of our player and monster? You can use this feature to visualize those properties. Next, we will look at the Show Velocities checkbox.

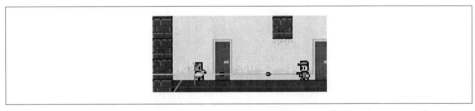

Figure 8-5. Toggle Show Velocities to see green lines that help visualize each entity's velocity as it moves.

Now, we can see the velocity projection for each entity including the player. This is helpful to see how velocity is affecting moving objects in the game. Try firing a grenade or jumping. Being able to see the velocity is incredibly helpful.

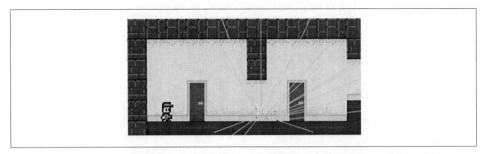

Figure 8-6. It's interesting to check out the velocity of each particle from a grenade's explosion.

The last feature of the debugger is the performance profiler. This is perhaps one of the most important tools in the debugger since it helps you visualize how long the draw, entity update, collision, and system lag take in milliseconds.

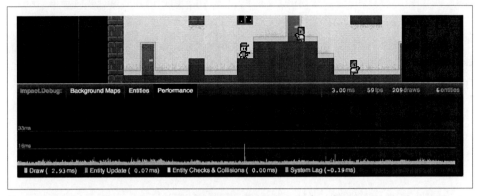

Figure 8-7. The profiler is a key tool to helping you visualize performance issues in your game.

The profiler lets us see a graph showing where the performance bottlenecks in your game are while you play it.

We have covered a lot in the building of your first game section. Right now, you should have a solid foundation of what it takes to make a game with Impact. Next, we will focus on how to publish your game.

Publishing Your Game

Once you have a finished game, you are going to want to publish it. Since we have been running our game in a local host, we could upload it as is and it should work online just fine. The one thing to keep in mind is that you don't want people to see your source code, and you don't want to accidentally distribute Impact's source. In order to package up our app, we use a technique called baking.

Baking Your Game

Baking will combine all your game files into a single file, which helps shorten the download time and compress the game.

You can run the bake script by doing the following:

Mac
> Open up a terminal window, navigate to the **tools/** directory, and write **./bake.sh**.

Windows
> For Windows, double-click the **bake.bat** file in the **tools/** directory. You also have to make sure that **bake.bat** can find **php.exe** on your system. You can either add the installation path of PHP to your PATH environment variable, or edit **bake.bat** to point directly to **php.exe**.

If you get an error message, make sure all the paths are correct. You can open **bake.bat** or **bake.sh** with a text editor. The only two lines you should ever need to change are these:

```
SET GAME=lib/game/main.jsSET OUTPUT_FILE=game.min.js
```

The `GAME` variable should point to your game's `main.js` file while the `OUTPUT_FILE` determines where the baked script file will be written.

If the script finishes without errors, you can find `game.min.js` in your Impact directory. You can now load this one .js file in your .html instead of the two files you had previously. Open up your index.html file and change the following lines:

```
<script type="text/javascript" src="lib/impact/impact.js"></script>
<script type="text/javascript" src="lib/game/main.js"></script>
```

to this:

```
<script type="text/javascript" src="game.min.js"></script>
```

Once you have correctly baked your game, you are ready to upload the `game.min.js` source file along with your media directory to your server. You should be able to upload your entire game exactly as you have been hosting it locally while testing. It's important to remember that your game's resources are being loaded through relative URLs, so in order to keep your game from breaking, make sure you keep everything in the same structure as you have it locally set up.

Mobile Web Support

While it is possible to also run Impact on mobile browsers, there are a lot of technical challenges, especially on Android devices, that make it difficult to cover in this book. Impact does come with some easy ways to test if your game is running on a mobile device. You can test the `ig.ua` class for the device type the game is running in. Here is a quick example for mobile:

```
if( ig.ua.mobile ) {
    // Disable sound for all mobile devices
    ig.Sound.enabled = false;
}
```

As you can see, Impact will let us know if the game is being played on a mobile device. It is also important to make sure that you set sound support to `false`, because most mobile browsers, including Safari on iOS, cannot play more than one sound at a time. Also, for browsers that don't support sound at all, you want to make sure your game doesn't try to load them or it may crash.

You can also use the `ig.ua` class to test if the game is running on the iPhone 4. This is important because of the iPhone's retina display. In this case, you will want to increase the game's scale like so:

```
if( ig.ua.iPhone4 ) {
    // The iPhone 4 has more pixels - we'll scale the
    // game up by a factor of 4
    ig.main('#canvas', MyGame, 60, 160, 160, 4);
}
else if( ig.ua.mobile ) {
    // All other mobile devices
    ig.main('#canvas', MyGame, 60, 160, 160, 2);
}
else {
    // Desktop browsers
    ig.main('#canvas', MyGame, 60, 240, 160, 2);
}
```

There is a lot to cover on running your game in mobile browsers, so read through Impact's documentation (*http://impactjs.com/documentation/impact-on-mobile-platforms*) for more details on handling iOS, adding mobile browser touch controls, and issues to watch out for.

Compiling for Native iOS

You can also distribute your game as a native iOS app. Impact comes with an Xcode project that you can use to compile a native iOS game. Everything you need to run the project is located in Impact's source in iOSImpact.zip. There is also a PDF with additional instructions. We'll take a quick look at how to copy over your game into the Xcode project and get it to compile.

In order to get this to work, you will need to register as a developer on Apple's site, which costs $100 annually. Once you are registered, you will need the latest version of Xcode. (In this book I am using Version 4.2.1 and OS X 10.7 (Lion).) You can use an older version of Xcode and OS X, but it is usually best to compile with the latest version of Xcode. It's also important to note that this is still an experimental feature, and at any point, Apple could start denying games created like this.

Unzip the iOSImpact.zip file and launch Xcode. Once you are in Xcode, click on Open Other… at the bottom of the welcome launcher.

Figure 8-8. Select Open Other from Xcode's welcome screen launcher.

Simply navigate to where you unzipped your iOSImpact project and open it up. You should see a screen similar to Figure 8-9.

While I am not going to be able to cover how Xcode works, I'll show you how to quickly get a build of the game up and running in the emulator. You'll see the project structure on the left. This contains all the Objective-C code needed to run Impact along with where your project's source code will go. Before we move your game over, let's take a quick look at getting this to run. Select a target device from the drop-down menu next to the run and stop buttons on the upper-left corner. I selected iPhone 5.0 Simulator.

Once you have the default target device selected, you can hit Run to compile the project. Xcode may show some issues in the output window, but none of them will keep the project from compiling. Once it's done building, you will see the default Impact game launch in the emulator.

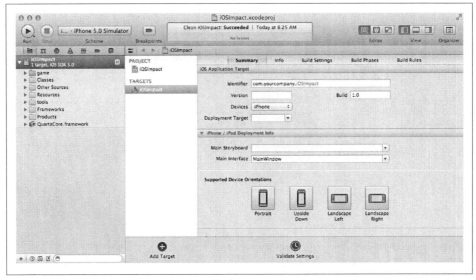

Figure 8-9. Our iOSImpact project in Xcode.

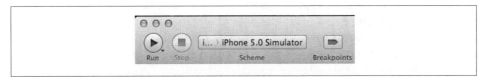

Figure 8-10. I selected iPhone 5.0 Simulator to test out the game.

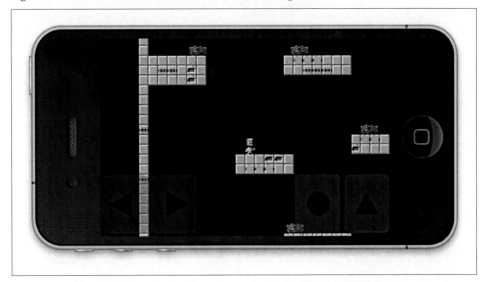

Figure 8-11. The default Impact sample game running in the iPhone 5.0 Simulator.

Now that we tested that Impact can compile, let's look at how to move our own game over to the Xcode project. If you go back to the project navigation window, you will see a game folder at the top of the project. This is where the JS code from your Impact game will be stored. If you open it up, everything should look familiar to you from when we originally set up our game.

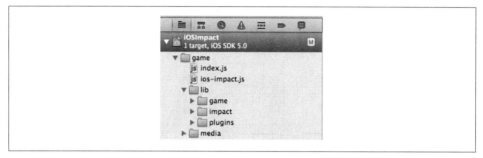

Figure 8-12. Our Impact game's JavaScript code lives inside of the game directory in the iOSImpact project.

At this point, you should be able to replace the contents of the game folder with your own game, along with the media folder with your game graphics, and recompile the project. To help you out, I have already created a special version of our game that is ready for iOS. From the book's source code folder, copy over the iOS ready **game** and **media** directory into your iOSImpact project. Once you have done that, run the project and you should see the game running in the emulator.

Figure 8-13. Our game running in the iOS emulator.

I'll highlight some of the changes I made to the source code to make it run on iOS.

First up, we need to include an iOS plugin in our game's **require** block:

```
'plugins.ios.ios'
```

This plugin is part of the iOSImpact project and includes all the logic needed to bridge the impact JS framework with Objective C.

I also had to change the resolution of our game to 240 × 160 and also scaled down some of the screen artwork to match the new resolution better:

```
ig.main( '#canvas', StartScreen, 60, 240, 160, 2 );
```

Next, our game needs to display some virtual buttons since there is no keyboard on iOS devices. There is a graphic for this already in our media folder. Simply create a new button property in your game classes that need to display buttons:

```
buttons: new ig.Image( 'media/buttons.png' ),
```

We can render them out in our draw method with the following code:

```
// Draw buttons
this.buttons.drawTile( 0, 110, 0, 80, 48, false, false );
this.buttons.drawTile( ig.system.width-80, 110, 1, 80, 48, false, false );
```

This creates two sets of buttons: the movement controls on the left and the jump/fire buttons on the right. Now, the last thing I had to do was set up touch controls. This is very easy to do by testing whether we are running the game in iOS:

```
init: function() {
    // Bind keys
    if( ios ) {
        // Add touch controls here
    }
    else {
        // Regular controls go here
    }
    // Rest of our init setup
},
```

Now we can switch over to touch controls when we run our game. Here is a quick example of how to bind to a touch area:

```
ig.input.bindTouchArea( 0, 224, 80, 96, 'left' );
ig.input.bindTouchArea( 80, 224, 80, 96, 'right' );
ig.input.bindTouchArea( 320, 224, 80, 96, 'shoot' );
ig.input.bindTouchArea( 400, 224, 80, 96, 'jump' );
```

As you can see, a touch area is simply a rectangle that fires off an event to the `ig.input` class when it detects that it is being pressed. Touch areas don't have any graphics associated with them, so we simply render the control images in the same location as our touch areas.

The final modification we needed to make was to the type of sound files we load in our iOS version of the game. By adding the following, we tell Impact to load iOS compatible .caf audio files:

```
if( ios ) {
    ig.Sound.use = [ig.Sound.FORMAT.CAF];
}
```

This goes right about our game constructor in the main.js module, just like we added the conditional to turn of sound in mobile browsers. In order to create .caf files, I simply exported the .mp3 sounds as .aff and changed the extension name to .caf.

So, this covers the basics of getting your game to run on iOS in Xcode. I also cleaned up the code a little and changed the text so it made more sense on the mobile devices instead of asking users to hit the space bar or keyboard keys. Make sure you check out the documentation that comes with the Impact iOS project to learn more about the process and review the iOS source code to see all of the modifications to our game's source code.

CHAPTER 9

Wrapping Up

I have covered a lot of information in this book and, if you are new to this process, it may take you some trial and error to get a feel for the best approach to building your own HTML5 games. I thought I would sum up a few of the things I have learned while making my own games:

- Have a clear plan on what platforms you intend to target. Try to understand the limitations of each such as performance issues on different browsers, especially around sound on mobile. Knowing the limitations can help you make informed decisions and architect better code.

- Start small and work your way up. You have to remember that even though Impact is able to run on almost all modern browsers, some of them may give you more issues than others. By starting simple and growing your game feature by feature, you can help alleviate some performance issues before it is too late. Also, don't expect to take an existing Impact game and have it run perfectly on a mobile device. You should test every step of the way.

- Finally, make sure to keep your project organized, especially when it comes to games that run on multiple platforms. Your mobile app will have icons, loading screens, embedded/loaded assets, and more. Try to keep these in folders that allow you to quickly find and modify on a platform-by-platform basis. This will help you in the long run when it comes to maintaining your project, especially if you need to do updates only on a specific platform at a time.

While there is no silver bullet for making a successful HTML5 game, hopefully this book has summed up all the core things you should think about when starting to make your own games with Impact. Luckily, Impact game development isn't very different from other 2D platforms such as Flash, so there is an incredible wealth of knowledge out there to help you take your code to the next level. Things such as AI, pathfinding, multiplayer networking, and more are simply a quick search or book away. Just don't get discouraged if your first game isn't an overnight hit; every game you make is a learning process. Eventually, you will stumble over something special and possibly create the next hit HTML5 game.

References and Links

While I tried to cover as much as I could in this book, there are a lot of great resources, links, and code samples out there to help you create your first Impact game. Here are a few worth checking out:

Simple button (https://gist.github.com/1395616)
> Looking to add simple buttons to your Impact game? Check out this code to help you.

A* path finding (https://gist.github.com/994534)
> A* path finding is incredibly helpful in top-down games when you need enemies or even the player to be able to move to a specific location on the map. This code will give you an idea of how to implement it in Impact.

Impact tutorial site (http://www.pointofimpactjs.com)
> This is a great resource for other Impact-related tutorials and code examples.

AppMobi (http://www.appmobi.com/?q=HTML5-game-dev-engine)
> AppMobi is a cloud-based mobile application development environment. They actually have a special bundle that comes with a license of Impact, which allows you to compile your game with a hardware-accelerated Canvas similar to how the iOS Impact project works. Also, make sure you check out their documentation at *http://www.appmobi.com/amdocs/lib/Tutorial-DirectCanvasWithImpactJS.pdf?r= 7039.*

Lawnchair (http://westcoastlogic.com/lawnchair/)
> This is a simple JSON data storage system to help you save game data locally to the player's browser.

Scoreoid (http://www.scoreoid.net/)
> Scoreoid is a multi-platform scoreboard API and more. If you are looking to add leader boards, stats, and even store game data in the cloud, make sure you check it out!

Bio Lab Entity Pack
> This set of source code comes with your license of Impact, and is an additional download. There are a lot of really good reference classes in here, so make sure you check it out when you set up your next game.

HTML5 Game Devs site (http://www.html5gamedevs.com)
> This is a great resource for staying up-to-date with the latest news and releases in the HTML5 game development world.

About the Author

For more than 13 years, Jesse Freeman has been on the cutting edge of interactive development with a focus on the Web and mobile platforms. As an expert in his field, Jesse has worked for VW, Tommy Hilfiger, Heavy, MLB, the New York Jets, HBO, and many more. Jesse was a traditional artist for most of his life until making the transition into interactive art, and he has never looked back.

Jesse is a Technical Architect/Technology Evangelist at Roundarch and is an active leader in New York's developer community. He is also active in the online community as a writer for several development sites including Adobe Developer Connection, O'Reilly Media, Inc., and Activetuts+. He can be found on Twitter at @jessefreeman. Jesse also speaks at conferences and does workshops, which you can find schedules for on his website at *http://jessefreeman.com*.

Get even more for your money.

Join the O'Reilly Community, and register the O'Reilly books you own. It's free, and you'll get:

- $4.99 ebook upgrade offer
- 40% upgrade offer on O'Reilly print books
- Membership discounts on books and events
- Free lifetime updates to ebooks and videos
- Multiple ebook formats, DRM FREE
- Participation in the O'Reilly community
- Newsletters
- Account management
- 100% Satisfaction Guarantee

Signing up is easy:

1. **Go to: oreilly.com/go/register**
2. **Create an O'Reilly login.**
3. **Provide your address.**
4. **Register your books.**

Note: English-language books only

To order books online:

oreilly.com/store

For questions about products or an order:

orders@oreilly.com

To sign up to get topic-specific email announcements and/or news about upcoming books, conferences, special offers, and new technologies:

elists@oreilly.com

For technical questions about book content:

booktech@oreilly.com

To submit new book proposals to our editors:

proposals@oreilly.com

O'Reilly books are available in multiple DRM-free ebook formats. For more information:

oreilly.com/ebooks

Spreading the knowledge of innovators   oreilly.com

The information you need, when and where you need it.

With Safari Books Online, you can:

Access the contents of thousands of technology and business books

- Quickly search over 7000 books and certification guides
- Download whole books or chapters in PDF format, at no extra cost, to print or read on the go
- Copy and paste code
- Save up to 35% on O'Reilly print books
- **New!** Access mobile-friendly books directly from cell phones and mobile devices

Stay up-to-date on emerging topics before the books are published

- Get on-demand access to evolving manuscripts.
- Interact directly with authors of upcoming books

Explore thousands of hours of video on technology and design topics

- Learn from expert video tutorials
- Watch and replay recorded conference sessions